How To Get
FREE PRESS

How To Get
FREE PRESS

by Toni Delacorte • Judy Kimsey • Susan Halas

A Do • It • Yourself Guide to Promote Your
Interests, Organizations or Business

Published in San Francisco by
HARBOR PUBLISHING

Distributed by G.P. Putnam's Sons

ISBN Cloth/ 0–936602–15–15
Jacket Design – Lynn Hollyn Associates
   Text Design/Composition – Haddon Craftsman
Text Printer and Binder – Fairfield Graphics
Copyeditor – Carol Dondrea

Table of Contents

Introduction:
Who are these people and why are they writing a book?

Authors Delacorte, Halas, and Kimsey all started their public relations careers as volunteers in assorted underfunded public interest and political campaigns.

In the beginning, we wrestled with questions like: What kind of information goes into a press release? When is the right time to call a press conference? What do I do if no one shows up? How do I get someone on a talk show? Is it better to sound serious and academic or darmatic and urgent? Who the heck can I contact? What can I do after I send a release to help make sure it is used?

We have written *How To Get Free Press* primarily to provide answers to these questions, and to help budding publicists both learn the basics and get better results from their efforts. These are people on limited budgets who are involved with a specific organization, a small business, an issue, a political campaign, or a special interest that appeals to a limited constituency. We want our book to demystify the process by which one can achieve maximum publicity for minimum money.

This book was also written for everyone who can relate to the experience that Judy Kimsey had when she first tried her hand at public relations:

"One spring day the members of a local consumer group decided to declare war on milk prices. Because I had always made A's in college English and journalism, I volunteered my services to write press releases and pamphlets for the cause, never dreaming what I was getting myself into. I was an amateur who suddenly had to deal with professionals, and the mere thought scared me to death. Somehow, I managed to muddle through with minimal damage to my self-esteem and the consumer movement."

In short, we all learned quickly that public relations was neither mysterious nor glamorous but that it did involve knowing and following basic rules, subscribing to certain ethical considerations, and doing a lot of hard work. We also learned through experience that knowing what to say to whom, in what way, and when, can produce spectacular results for a small commercial venture, a young politico, or anyone's favorite cause. It was our intention to write a book based on our collective thirty years of knowledge and experience that would inform our novice associates of some of the correct ways to achieve those results.

How To Get Free Press is, essentially, the sort of book that we wish had been around when we began: a book that outlines the basic how-to information by first providing the fundamental tools (the *who, what, where, when,* and *why*) and then citing specific examples of publicity efforts in four different areas.

Because every PR campaign strategy differs from every other, depending on the issues, products, or people involved, we cannot claim that this book will answer every question or provide the solution to every problem. However, we feel that through our experiences in getting publicity for many diverse groups and interests (including wine, whales, women, and lots in between), we have learned basic rules that can be applied to almost every aspect of public relations.

We pass these along, hoping they might better prepare others about to engage in the battle for media attention.

We also hope to encourage people to have fun, be creative, and develop their own unique styles. Things would be pretty boring if everyone said the same things in the same way.

While not everyone can produce a rip-roaring, mind-blowing PR campaign that gets covered by the press around the world, almost anyone can learn to write a press release or to book someone on a talk show. All it takes is knowing how to communicate with the media in a way that both interests and makes sense to them. In this book, we explain how different media work and we examine the various approaches one might use to get the best results.

It isn't necessary to have a degree in communications to be an effective publicist. Some of the best people in the field were originally housewives, retirees, or out-of-work free-lance writers. It is only necessary to have a good typewriter, a telephone, and quick access to a copy machine, the library, and the post office. Then, armed with enthusiasm, ethics, and a raison d'etre, it is possible to generate effective publicity for just about anything.

Somewhere out there, there is a reporter waiting to hear from you. Go to it and good luck.

SECTION I

WHO?
WHAT?
WHEN?
WHERE?
WHY?

1
WHO? A Brief Analysis of Editors, Reporters, and Other Media Types

Since God invented them, journalists have been asking: who, what, when, where, and sometimes why. These, therefore, are the questions that all good public relations people must learn to answer in one form or another. More importantly, these questions provide a learning format for novice publicists: Who should be contacted in the media? What kinds of materials are sent? Why is PR a valid, viable concept? When are events scheduled and press releases sent out, and when is coverage best? Where is the best place for a staged event? How does the publicist handle the physical space? What problems are involved when "where" is out in the boonies?

Let's start at the beginning. Perhaps "who" is the most overwhelming aspect of public relations to the novice. One must wade through a huge number of functionaries—assignment editors, producers, city desk people, public affairs directors, and so on—in order to accomplish anything. Trying to figure out who to call for what reason has undoubtedly kept many headache and ulcer doctors in business.

However, identifying the correct entity isn't as difficult as it seems. Let's take a look at Who's Who in Media.

EDITORS (PRINT MEDIA)

Editors from the top down are mostly concerned with the following questions: Is this story consistent with our format and editorial policy? If it is, will it be interesting to a large number of people? Are we first with it? How long will it take to do? Is the research already done? Do we have a reporter who knows something about this subject? Will it sell papers, or increase our prestige?

When you talk or write to an editor, be flexible. Go in with several different angles on the story. Editors like to feel they have made an executive decision by choosing the story angle. They don't like being told how the story should be written. Phrase the story request in a way that makes it hard to say no: "Would you rather do this or that? Would you rather interview a man or a woman? Would the beginning of the week be better than the end?"

Editors are the ones with most control over ideas and content. They are not beholden to their publisher, the advertisers, or to any organization. It is worth noting, however, that some publications, such as entertainment guides and certain small weekly papers, will not even consider giving editorial space or news coverage to any profit organization or business unless the organization has bought ads in the publication or has promised to do so in the future.

Editors also assign the reporter who will cover a story. They almost never write a story themselves, but they often rewrite, changing tone or emphasis, deleting or adding sections, and generally guiding the article from the idea stage through publication.

Therefore, you should get to know how editors think. Get background information from friendly reporters or from anyone else who can help you determine how to deal with the editor.

Since editors assign writers, it is possible to suggest a reporter for your story. Never make demands on an editor, but simply suggest that so-and-so did a good job covering a similar story, or is familiar with the background information on this story. You can be direct or indirect depending on how well you get along with the editor in question.

Sometimes editors are enemies. They hate what you're talking about. They hate your organization. They hate the idea that you are trying to use them to sell your product. They hate you. In this case, forget it. Don't waste time with people who block stories. There are many media outlets in America and you can always find someone else. The idea is to get coverage, not to engage in philosophical argument over coverage. Keep shopping, don't get discouraged.

Let's look now at specific types of editors.

EXECUTIVE EDITOR:

Executive editors are responsible for the whole newspaper, in the philosophical as well as the money-making sense. They don't have much contact with the day-to-day operations, unless a subject appears that is close to their own or the publisher's heart. They occasionally take an active role in major national stories initiated by the paper, as well as helping to set editorial policy. In all likelihood, the novice publicist will not deal with an executive editor.

MANAGING EDITOR:

This is the highest editor on the operational level. Managing editor's hire and fire, supervise the content of the paper, and take flack for mistakes. They are usually busy and hard to see. Don't be surprised if it takes a month to set an appointment.

CITY EDITOR:

This is the pivotal position—the person in charge of assigning staff and deciding which stories will be covered on a given day. City editors are the key people for the publicist. Get to know them, and be considerate of their time. Most city editors are either young hot-shots on the way up or older people who like the power of the position.

SUNDAY/WEEKEND EDITORS:

The Sunday paper usually has a somewhat different staff from the weekday crew. And it may have a Sunday editor, who is in charge of the whole shebang or at least of the longer features.

Sunday papers often take free-lance material, and will sometimes run current reprints from another paper outside of their circulation area. For instance, if a terrific piece appeared in last week's *Chicago Sun-Times* on a subject dear to your organization's heart, clip the item, send it to the local Sunday editor, and suggest that it might be interesting to run the story with a side bar (side story) on the local angle. Your organization, of course, is the local angle.

Most Sunday magazines have about six weeks lead time. Start talking to Sunday editors about 10–12 weeks ahead of the desired publication date for a story, especially if color photos are involved. And remember that, except for the front news section, the bulk of most Sunday papers gets printed on Thursday night.

SECTION EDITORS:

The Home, Business, Sports, and Entertainment sections normally have their own special editors. These sections usually have a specific amount of space in both the daily and Sunday papers. And it is the section editor who assigns the allotted space. If coverage would be most helpful in the Business section, send the release to to the business editor. A business-oriented release sent to the city desk is not automatically going to get to the Business section. A news editor looks for stories that are pegged to a date. A section editor looks for material pegged to a certain subject or audience. If it can be written and run any time over the next year, so much the better.

When trying to interest a section editor in a story, remember that it isn't necessary for the whole story to focus on you or what you're doing. For example, if the subject is health care in minority communities, chances are that several groups are working in this area. Suggest a story on the subject of community health care, and have your organization participate in the interview. This tact increases visibility of the problem, and wins friends among other organizations. In short, everyone benefits.

PHOTO EDITORS:

In the modern scheme of things, the photo editor is on the way out. Most picture magazines have folded. Photo people tend to work for word people who, in turn, work for business people.

If there is a photo editor, he or she will assign the photographer for the story. If a photographer isn't assigned, arrange to have someone else take photos. Stories with photos are much more attractive to editors.

WRITERS

After the editors come the writers. These are the people that the publicist deals with most frequently.

REPORTERS AND FREE-LANCERS

Reporters and free-lance writers are entirely different from editors. They come in both sexes, and they are usually younger. Also, unless they are just hacks, they usually have some personal involvement with a story. They want to do a good job because their name is on the finished product, and they want to be recognized and rewarded for their work. They want to be assigned good stories, and they want their stories to get past the editors unchanged—which is not always possible.

Get to know these writers by making personal visits to meet them and by keeping track of their stories. Make contacts ahead of time—don't wait for an emergency.

Be nice to reporters and free-lancers. They have all the talent, and are at the bottom of the pecking order. Treat them like people. Take them home for dinner and introduce them to your family. They are basically competitive, curious people who want recognition and an interesting life. Be warned, however, that while reporters may be sympathetic, they will not put themselves in an advocacy position. And even though free-lance writers can and sometimes do take sides, it is still the job of both types to report what they see and hear the way they see and hear it, which will not necessarily be word for word what you told them.

Try to avoid off-the-record conversations. Something either can or cannot be talked about. If something can't be discussed, simply say "We haven't reached a decision on that. I'll call you when we have a little more information." Basically, don't tell reporters anything you don't want the world to know, and don't tell them how to write or interpret a story.

EDITORIAL WRITERS:

Editorial writers are in media ivory towers. They do not have the usual time and deadline pressures other media writers face. Often they have been moved into editorials because there can be only one managing editor and one executive editor, and senior writers have to be promoted someplace.

The head of the editorial section is a good person to know even if it is apparent from the beginning that the two of you will agree on nothing in this life. Editorial writers thrive on arguments. They will judge entire organizations on the quality of the arguments the organizations present over a period of months or years. Even if they ignore or make fun of your organization, after a while they often steer you to people in their own publication with more respect for your ideas than they have.

Editorial writers are among the few people in modern society who actually keep up with the rest of the world. So if you are planning a benefit in support of exploited sugar workers in Costa Rica, it is a good idea to call up your favorite and most conservative editorial writer to see if he knows anything you don't about the subject. Part of the publicist's job is avoiding surprises, especially unpleasant surprises. And one of the best way's to accomplish this goal is to test arguments on an editorial writer whose chief delight in life is picking your position full of holes. Get to know these writers. They have friends, and they can and will help.

BEAT WRITERS:

Certain writers specialize in certain subjects, such as education, science, urban affairs, transportation, City Hall, and state government. These are all typical beats. If your area of concern falls into one or more of these categories it is in your best interest to know the writer who regularly covers it.

Beat writers are a good source of information about your subject in the outside world. They often know of parallel trends in other places, for example. Because the subject is their specialty they read the trade press and the academic press, they attend mettings, and they become quite well informed. They also have wide contacts in the field.

Sometimes, however, they also have strong personal prejudices. If a beat writer gives you or your organization consistently unfair or unsympathetic treatment, first try to work it out. Next approach others with your material. Of course, establishing rapport with a beat writer makes both your lives easier.

BUREAUS:

A bureau is the office of a publication, wire service or network (both radio and television news) that is located in a different city from the home or main office. The New York Times and other daily newspapers have bureaus in many other cities. So do United Press International, Associated Press, ABC-TV news, and a host of other biggies. People who run the bureaus are called bureau chiefs. Other people who work in the office are called correspondents. Free-lancers who are occasionally assigned by a local bureau to cover stories are called stringers.

The above people include photographers, camera crews and radio reporters as well as writers.

CORRESPONDENTS:

People who work for the bureau are called correspondents. People who work for the bureau on an occasional or part time basis are called stringers.

Correspondents and stringers are usually assigned by the bureau chief in their region, who in turn is usually guided by the main office. Unfortunately, the main office is usually oblivious to anything happening outside of its immediate area. One way to get around any possible disinterest is to deal directly with the main office and the person in charge. The main office can always overrule the bureau but never the reverse. If a generous budget is available, pick up the phone and call the main office, wherever it is. People are still impressed by long distance phone calls.

ELECTRONIC MEDIA

Sloppy use of the English language has resulted in an ambiguous definition of the term *media.* Originally, *media* meant radio and TV. However, over the years the term has evolved to include print. Now, in order to differentiate radio and TV from the "print media," one must use the term *electronic media.* In this book, we follow the popular trend and use *media* to include everything, and *electronic media* to specify radio and television.

Because of the nature of electronics, both radio and television have a few job positions different from those in print media. These people are often critical to a PR campaign's success.

NEWS DIRECTORS

Television news directors are similar to executive editors in the print media. They make decisions about the "look" of their news and the personnel, but rarely are they contacted about a specific story.

Radio news directors, on the other hand, are the people most likely to decide whether to use your story or interview, or to cover your event for their newscasts. Most radio stations (except those with all-news formats or those affiliated with big networks) have a small news staff—usually one director and a couple of reporters. Thus, it is always best to contact the radio news director either by phone or a written press release about getting news coverage on his or her station.

ASSIGNMENT EDITORS

Without a doubt, these people are the most important contacts in the television news department. As their title implies, assignment editors (AE's) assign particular reporters to particular stories, and actually decide what locally based stories their station will cover.

Since there are different AE's for the 6 P.M. and the 11 P.M. news shows, you will have to get to know who is who. For the noon news, the best contact is the producer as this time slot is usually used to rehash or update the previous night's news.

In any medium- to large-sized metropolitan community, an AE has the difficult task of deciding which 20 or 30 stories, from among hundreds of possibilities, the station will cover. These possibilities may include as many as 300 press releases, phone calls, tips, communications via the police radio, possible local angles to national news stories, suggestions from reporters, and so on—all contributing to the mix of "what's going on out there" that the station might want to report on.

Assignment editors are busy, harried people under a great deal of pressure; they don't have time to listen to long explanations. They want to know in as few words as possible what is going on where and at what time. Reporters want to know interesting or colorful background information—AE's do not.

If you are doing something that you think might be of interest to television news and don't have time to send a press release, it's perfectly all right to call an assignment editor. It's also a good idea to let these editors know when they can expect to get the best and most relevant shots (remember, television is primarily pictures explained by words). This is crucial if you are planning an event that may be going on for several hours or all day. Make sure to tell the AE when the best action is likely to occur.

TELEVISION NEWS PRODUCERS:

Although morning, afternoon, evening and late night news shows may share the same assignment editors, each show usually has its own producer, especially in major market areas.

The producers to know are those doing the noon news and the late evening news. Working with less staff and less leeway, these people are expected to produce a news broadcast that is significantly different from the major 6 P.M. edition. They have a hard job, and they deserve your help and consideration. Also, keep in mind that the noon news is one of the few news programs that will schedule a live guest or spot interview, especially if it can be filmed in advance.

Most locally produced noon news radio and TV shows also have their own producer, who must be contacted in order to place a guest on the show. Sometimes these producers will have a large number of guest possibilities and be brusque to the point of rudeness with you. At other times—especially if you've gotten to know them—they may actually call you and ask if there is a new angle that might be of interest to their viewers or listeners.

Get to know producers—their interests and technical needs. They are helpful beings.

DOCUMENTARY AND FEATURE TV PRODUCERS

Nowadays most locally produced television programming is related to regular newscasts and public affairs and/or talk shows. Documentary and special feature or investigative units are few and far between, as local stations are putting less money into these kinds of efforts. However, if local stations have them, get to know them.

There are advantages to getting coverage outside the news: "Specials" are usually aired in prime time slots; they may be promoted by the station, aired by affiliate stations in other markets, and in general give better and deeper coverage to a subject than is possible on the news.

If you think what you're doing might interest a special feature producer on your local station or even on one of the networks, don't hesitate to send a letter and follow up with a phone call to discuss the possibilities.

BROADCAST PUBLIC AFFAIRS:

While broadcast public affairs departments should be concerned with keeping their listening and viewing public informed on critical issues of the day, they often fall woefully short of meeting that obligation.

Unfortunately, public affairs has the lowest priority, worst time slots, and smallest budgets of any department. A FCC survey showed that the bulk of public affairs programming is aired between midnight and 4 A.M., or between church shows on Sundays. The recent deregulation of the broadcast industry means that these problems will probably get worse before—and if—they get better.

Public affairs directors are, however, in need of interesting material from local people. Many radio stations produce short programs that deal with topics of concern to the community—politics, the environment, crime, health, and so on. They are often interested in "how-to" type information. So even if you are in a commercial business, you may have some good tips to share with listeners in your community. The best way to find out what programs or opportunities are available is to call the public affairs department and ask for a list or get a verbal description of all shows that feature guests either in pretaped interviews (in-studio or by phone) or live call-in talk shows.

The best approach is to call the producer of the show or the public affairs director and explain who you are and whom you represent and that your client can talk about the subject on a particular date. This is the fastest way to determine whether there is immediate interest, possible interest (they'll call you back), or no interest whatsoever.

TALK SHOW PRODUCERS

Talk show producers may work independently from the public affairs department. It is important to know that it is not very productive to call the host of a talk show directly (unless it is someone you know well or unless that person is also the producer). To find out who to contact, call the station and simply ask for the name of the producer of the show.

Getting yourself or a spokesperson from your organization or business on a show is much easier than you might expect. Again, just a quick phone call describing what might be of interest to the audience will usually—or at least, often—produce successful results.

HOW TO APPROACH PEOPLE IN THE MEDIA

Although there are other people the publicist will have to deal with occasionally, those just described are the main ones. The next question is how to set up contacts with these people. Media contacts are perhaps the most important tool of the publicist. Without them, little is accomplished.

Begin by making a list of the functionaries—editors, writers, producers, and so on—who may be interested in your story. Call them and arrange for an appointment, a luncheon, or an after-work drink. Face-to-face contact establishes you as a person rather than a voice.

At the first meeting, don't ramble on about your subject unless the editor, writer, or whomever expresses a fervid interest. Instead, ask a lot of questions: What are the deadlines? The newspaper's or station's interests? What about photos? Who is good at covering this area? And so on. Ask every question a beginner would ask. There's no crime in it. In fact, novices get gentler treatment than do professionals, who are already supposed to know the ropes. Everyone likes to be a guru and help a newcomer. Play that angle for all it's worth.

Be on the lookout for people who think for themselves, who see different angles, and who are curious, responsive, and open to new ideas.

Work hard to retain contacts. Don't be a pest. Do present good stories and solid information. Some contacts will become personal friends, others will be avoided at all costs.

Remember that psychology plays a role in media work. As with everyone, the people you will deal with have biases and prejudices. It will help you, therefore, to become aware of their mentalities. It is easier to cope with an attitude that is known and understood than to be faced with one that is totally unexpected.

This is the who in media. The next question a good reporter asks is "What?"

2
What? The Basic Types of Media Materials, How They Are Used, and Examples

After establishing who one contacts, the next question is with what does one contact them? When is a press release sent out instead of a calendar announcement? What do you say to all of those editors and writers? What *is* public relations?

Public relations is the art of creating news by careful production and selective placement of editorial material. It is used to raise consciousness, mobilize public opinion, apply pressure, expand participation, raise money, increase credibility, and create an image. It can be used in a commercial sense to get people to attend an event, shop at a particular store, patronize a particular restaurant, or use a certain service.

In PR, attention and space are synonymous. The more space you get, the more attention you get. There are two types of space in media: paid space, which is called advertising, and editorial space, which is essentially "free press."

Editorial space is what concerns the publicist. It consists of news stories, features, public affairs programming, editorials, talk shows, free speech messages, columns, reviews, and interviews. And, it isn't as hard to come by as one might think.

Publicists and reporters belong to a mutual admiration society. Without people out there calling up reporters and editors with fast-breaking news, without various organizations issuing press releases, the 6 o'clock news would be pretty boring. By the same token, organizations, events, and people periodically experience a wild desire to go public, which can only be done via the media. It is the publicist's job to make sure that the interaction between the media and those covered flows like Morton's salt on a rainy day. To do this, it is necessary to capture the gist of a story in as little space as possible, making life a little easier for harassed editors and reporters. Spare them the sloppy, single-spaced, five-page press release. It's likely to end up in the garbage instead of on the front page, and you are likely to be ignored forevermore.

WHAT IS NEWS?

It is critical for the publicist to understand the concept of news: News is anything that is of interest to people. It comes in two varieties—hard and soft. Hard news is what you get on the front page of the paper and what you hear as the lead story on the 6 o'clock news. Something big has happened today. The "today" is important: Yesterday is not news; today is. Likewise, something *happens* in hard news—usually something of major importance. Finally, hard news is fact. Opinions belong on the editorial page, not page one.

Soft news is also called "feature news," or more rudely, "fluff." It can occur over an extended period. It can have a smattering of opinion. The article itself may include a great deal of background and history.

An example will differentiate hard from soft news. A consumer group filing suit against a nursing home for mistreatment resulting in an elderly patient's death is hard news. A good publicist will call a press conference to bring attention to the fact. It is hard news because (1) it is timely—the filing is occurring *today;* (2) something is *happening*—a suit is being filed; (3) there are hard facts involved—the suit is being filed, and the consumer group is showing evidence to back their accusation.

A soft news story on the same general topic might cover the overall plight of the elderly, citing specific case histories and interviews with a number of people and organizations. The publicist will arrange the interviews and prepare any background materials that will be helpful to the reporter. This story could run as a side bar (alongside) to the news story, or it could be a separate feature.

TOOLS OF PUBLIC RELATIONS

What tools does one use to place the news in the proper editorial space? The list is long. In the following section, a brief definition is given for various written materials, and one clear example is given for each. *All PR materials should be double spaced.* This is one rule that should never be broken, and one that will let an editor know immediately if he or she is dealing with a professional or an amateur. Even though you are in the latter category, there is no need to announce the fact. What they don't know won't hurt them—or you.

All written material must contain the name, address, and phone number of your organization, plus a contact name and phone number at the top.

Most materials also contain a release line (the date the information can be published) and a headline that tells who, what, when, and where. With the exception of the op-ed article whose length is predetermined by the newspaper, each of the written materials discussed here should be kept to a single sheet of paper, although a release can sometimes run longer. Keep the copy clear, simple, and clean. Make sure that the facts are accurate. And, again, double space.

The following materials are divided into three basic categories: individual items released to the press, press kit materials, and internal organizational material.

INDIVIDUAL ITEMS

The first group of press materials consists of specific items that are *usually* (but not always) released individually.

The Press Release

Along with the basic information, a press release contains a release line. If the information can be used at once, enter "For Release Upon Receipt" or "For Immediate Release" near the contact's name in capital letters. If the information cannot be released immediately, add the date the story can be used. Or give the date after which the story *cannot* be used.

Next, write a headline. If the subject of the release is a scheduled news event, the headline should provide the reporter with all information necessary to arrive at the correct place at the correct time, with some idea of what is going on—the good old who, what, why, when, and where.

The first paragraph reiterates and expands the headline. The second paragraph provides additional information about important speakers, sponsors, background, and the like. The third paragraph identifies the organization and its past activities.

A press release should be written as if it were going to be published word for word in the newspaper, or read over the air. The tone of the release should be straight and factual. Except when writing for coming theatrical attractions, avoid adjectives like "terrific." Stay away from loaded words like *racist, male chauvinist, capitalist,* or anything else that sounds as though you are passing judgment. Even if the term is descriptive and accurate, it is stylistically inappropriate for a press release.

Try not to predict exactly how many or who may show up at an event. Use words like *expect* and *anticipate.* You can't be sure how many irate mothers will appear to protest the closing of the free baby clinic, but you can "expect" hundreds. For that matter, you can "expect" thousands, but for future credibility, keep expectations in some proximity to reality. If obscure facts are being cited, provide a source.

There is virtually no situation that requires a press release longer than two pages. A press release is limited to one event. If two events are scheduled, write separate releases, since assignment editors file correspondence by date.

Notification of Press Conference or Event

Sometimes the notification of a press conference or other media event takes the form of a press release, but usually it does not include details. It should simply state what is happening, when, and where, and should be mailed approximately a week before the event. After three or four days, call up and make sure that it has been received. Ask if you can answer any questions, but don't let the cat out of the bag—don't tell what it is about —before the conference or event.

NOTIFICATION OF
PRESS CONFERENCE   CONTACT: Judy Kimsey
TUESDAY, OCTOBER 28, 9:30 A.M.
123 MAIN STREET (AT ELM)
OAKLAND, CALIFORNIA

CITIZEN'S GROUP FILES COMPLAINTS AGAINST MAJOR LENDING INSTITUTIONS: REDLINING.

California Citizen Action Group will lodge formal complaints against six major lending institutions on Tuesday, October 28. A press conference will be held at CalCag headquarters, 123 Main Street at 9:30 A.M. to substantiate redlining charges against Central Bank, Chartered Bank of London, Lloyd's Bank, Security Pacific, Security National Bank, and United California Bank.

FOR IMMEDIATE
RELEASE   CONTACT: Toni Delacorte
TUESDAY, NOVEMBER 15, 1977

JANE FONDA TO HOST SF BENEFIT PREMIERE OF "JULIA" ON NOVEMBER 17

Jane Fonda, star of the new motion picture, "JULIA", will be on hand for the film's San Francisco Premiere on Thursday, November 17 at the Metro Theatre on Union Street. The Premiere will benefit SOLARCAL, a project of the California Public Policy Center, which would develop solar energy in the public interest in the state of California.

Ms. Fonda will be at the theatre starting at 7P.M. that evening. She will also attend a champagne reception at the Delancey Street Restaurant (directly across the street from the theatre) after the 7:30 performance.

-30-

NOTE TO
ASSIGNMENT EDITORS: Ms. Fonda will be available for short interviews in the lobby of the theatre after the film has begun (approx. 7:30P.M.)—if you are interested in a one—on—one at this time, please schedule it with Toni Delacorte (397-6300).

FOR IMMEDIATE
RELEASE   CONTACT: Toni Delacorte
September 9, 1975   Sam Hurst

HAYDEN SAYS TUNNEY'S DROP IN FIELD POLL
DUE TO FAILURE ON KEY ISSUES

Tom Hayden, candidate for the Democratic nomination for U.S. Senate, said today that Senator John V. Tunney's dramatic 10 per cent erosion of support in the latest Field Public Opinion Poll is the result of Tunney's abandonment of the rank and file of the Democratic party.

"The Field Poll shows above all that Tunney can be defeated," Hayden said from his Santa Monica headquarters. "He is only 6 per cent from losing majority support from his own party. His stand in opposition to National Health Care, his support for the deregulation of natural gas, and his support of high level military spending are antagonizing the traditional rank and file of the Democratic party," Hayden said.

Of his own gain in the Field Poll, Hayden said, "The three per cent rise from 13 per cent to 16 per cent is very good. My growing support indicates the campaign is being taken seriously, my candidacy is viable, and we have achieved our summer goal of building a stable statewide organization. I expect this trend to continue during the coming months until Tunney falls," Hayden said.

Calendar or Public Service Announcement (PSA)

Most newspapers carry a calendar of upcoming events. Radio and television stations provide the same service as what they may call a "Community Calendar," or as a public service announcement (PSA).

Both calendar releases and PSA's contain only the basic information—who, what, why, when and where—of the event. Do not rhapsodize or get carried away with adjectives. This is a *listing,* not an ad or endorsement.

Check local television and radio stations for the length required for PSA's. Most stations have 10-, 20-, 30-, or 60-second spots. Since the announcer may read your copy directly if it is well composed, type the word *Announcer,* and then proceed with the message, typed all in capital letters so that it can be read easily. Needless to say, double space.

CALENDARS

Calendars are listings of coming events in your area. Sometimes they are called the "Datebook" or "Community Bulletin Board," but basically they all list future events, be they entertainment, political events, lectures, benefits, or what have you.

All calendars have deadlines, and those deadlines are often much further in advance than you would think. For instance the deadline for the Sunday calendar of the main newspaper in your area is likely to be two Thursdays before the Sunday. Obviously, bi-weekly and monthly calendars have an even longer lead time. Newspapers also often have daily calendars. In many places the deadline for these is three working days prior to the date of publication. It may be different where you are, so call to be sure.

Write your calendar, announcement send it in by the deadline, and call to check that it has been received. If you want a featured position, send clearly identified black and white photos that show someone or something relevant to the event. They should be no larger than 8 × 10. Your pictures will usually not be returned, so don't send anything of personal or sentimental value.

If you live in a city that attracts a lot of tourists, don't forget to send your listings to the free "what to do" magazines.

Radio calendars are the same except they are written to time.

COMMUNITY CALENDAR
ANNOUNCEMENT   CONTACT: Toni Delacorte
FOR RELEASE: THRU FEB. 23, 1980

CARNIVAL OF DANCE SPECTACULAR: FRIDAY, FEBRUARY 23 AT THE GALLERIA

THE CARNIVAL OF DANCE, an evening of artistic achievement, non-stop entertainment and dancing, will take place on Friday, February 23 at the Galleria, 101 Kansas Street, San Francisco, 8P.M. The audience is invited to dance the night away or just watch while twelve San Francisco dance companies perform to a disco beat. Tickets are $15 and are available through BASS outlets, the Record Factory, Liberty House and Bullock's. All proceeds will benefit the performing artists and the Support Services for the Arts. For more information, dial TELETIX.

PUBLIC SERVICE ANNOUNCEMENTS

PSA's are simple announcements that usually air on radio and television. A good PSA campaign is time-consuming, has a long lead time, and can get excellent results at virtually no cost. Public service announcements cannot be used to solicit funds or take a political viewpoint. But they can be used to call attention to your activities and services.

For good PSA results, find out who at the stations decides what goes on the air and how much lead time they require. Write and produce the announcement to specified length and submit it by the deadline. If you have an ongoing campaign, especially if it's informational—consumer hints, things to know before signing a lease, the seven danger signals for VD, and the like—send the whole series in at one time, so the stations can choose which ones to broadcast when.

Stations have a lot to pick from. But while they receive loads of public service material from such national organizations as the American Cancer Society and the Ad Council, they are very receptive to interesting, locally generated information because it has more direct interest to their listening audience. Take time, therefore, to make your information interesting to people in your community. Some stations will help you tape, others will want only the script, and still others will help you produce fairly sophisticated spots with music and sound effects. As you get to know your stations, you will find out who can be helpful.

PSA's usually go through the public affairs department, but have to be cleared at some higher level. This takes time. However, after a station has aired 1 or 2 of your PSA's, the lead time can be cut considerably because they know you. Again, that's why it is important to establish your credibility before an emergency comes up. Often it's a good idea to send a cover letter that gives some background on your organization.

CONTACT: Judy Kimsey

FOR USE THROUGH APRIL 23, 1981
PUBLIC SERVICE ANNOUNCEMENT: 30 sec.

BOOGIE WITH THE BARD AND HELP LAUNCH THE
BERKELEY SHAKESPEARE FESTIVAL'S 1981 SEASON
ON FRIDAY, APRIL 24 AT THE SHATTUCK HOTEL IN
BERKELEY. A LIVE SWING BAND BEGINS THE CELE-
BRATION OF SHAKESPEARE'S BIRTHDAY AT 8:00
P.M. TICKETS ARE $4 AT THE DOOR. WEAR A COS-
TUME, BRING A FRIEND, AND JOIN THE FESTIVI-
TIES ON FRIDAY, APRIL 24.

Free Speech Messages

A free speech message is time-consuming to write and place, but good ones more than repay the effort. They are especially rewarding because they can trigger response and feedback in the form of letters, and phone calls, as well as personal recognition for the speaker.

It is a good idea to write the free speech message while the person or people who are actually going to give it are present. Have these people talk about their thoughts and feelings, and write this material down verbatim. Notice the speech patterns. Pull out the phrases that are direct and to the point and discard the rest. Keep the sentences short and easy to say, and keep reworking it until it exactly fits the delivery style of the speaker.

You must write it according to the time and space requirements of the paper or station. If it is for broadcast, the station will need a copy of the script in advance of the taping date. The top of the script should also contain the name and address of the organization, date, contact and phone number, name of speaker, phone, occupation, and the exact length of time the script runs.

When taping a free speech message for television, don't wear white or clothes with a busy geometric pattern. Take off your glasses if you possibly can. Follow the directions of the producer and/or technical crew.

Relax. If you are nervous, consciously slow down, rather than allowing yourself to unconsciously speed up. Fear often makes even low pitched voices sound shrill or wobbly, so practice.

ELECTRICITY AND GAS
FOR PEOPLE (E&GP)   Contact:
"Turn PG&E around. . . ."   Media: Susan Halas
212 Fair Oaks
San Francisco, Ca. 94110   Other: Mike Miller

PUBLIC OPINION MESSAGE/FREE SPEECH
MESSAGE *60 Seconds*

AFTER ELEVEN RATE INCREASES LAST YEAR PG&E IS ASKING THE STATE PUBLIC UTILITIES COMMISSION TO INCREASE YOUR GAS & ELECTRICITY RATES AGAIN TO THE TUNE OF $233 MILLION, WHICH WILL COST THE AVERAGE HOUSEHOLD AN ADDITIONAL $40/YEAR IN UTILITIES BILLS.

WE'VE HAD ENOUGH. NOW IT'S TIME FOR THE LITTLE GUY TO TALK BACK. THAT'S WHY WE'VE ORGANIZED THE CAMPAIGN TO TURN PG&E AROUND. IF YOU'RE TIRED OF PAYING MORE AND MORE, JOIN WITH US IN PROTESTING THE RATE HIKES TO THE PUBLIC UTILITIES COMMISSION AT THEIR HEARINGS ON FEBRUARY 4TH, 5TH AND 6TH.

FOR MORE INFORMATION, CALL ELECTRICITY AND GAS FOR PEOPLE (E&GP) 648-6402, OR IN THE EAST BAY, 658-4834 (THOSE NUMBERS AGAIN 648-6402, EAST BAY, 658-4834). STOP THE RATE INCREASE. ELECTRICITY AND GAS FOR PEOPLE. TURN PG&E AROUND.

RADIO AND TV EDITORIALS BY THE MANAGEMENT AND EDITORIAL REBUTTALS

Almost all of the larger radio and TV stations run management-written editorials on topics of the day. These editorials are usually produced by the public affairs or news department. Depending on the size of the station editorials may be written by one person or by editorial committee.

If you want a station to do one editorial or a series on a given subject, it is usually a good idea to call the person in charge of editorials and discuss the subject. Does it interest them? Do they foresee themselves taking a position on it? Remember, when you talk about broadcast editorials, you are talking about a broad general audience. After the calls send a letter recapping what has been discussed.

Within a week you should know if the station has decided to run an editorial. If their stance is favorable to your view, all well and good. If it is unfavorable, the equal time rule applies to all broadcasters, and you may request a similar amount of time to present a rebuttal. From the viewpoint of access, then, it doesn't really matter whether they are for you or against you. If they comment at all, your position will get air time.

When you write a rebuttal it is important to remember that this time is *your* time. It may be the only time you get on that station to present your side of the story. Don't waste it by calling attention to the arguments your opponents have presented. Instead, present your own best case, and call attention to opposition arguments only when they are factually in error and you have evidence to prove it. Otherwise, trying to counter false allegations only circulates them to a wider audience.

If you have approached many stations about editorials, and they all go against you, you will have a lot of rebuttals to write. Make them all different and use a different person to give each one. It takes time but it works well. And keep in mind that credibility is the single most important ingredient in rebuttals, and race, accent, class, and affiliation all influence perception —especially on television.

PROPOSITION "L"

When San Francisco Street Sweepers were asking for $17,000 a year, it made national news. But that was just a small example of what is wrong with City salaries.

Because of weaknesses in the City Charter, most pay rates are the result of political power applied by unions on elected officials. Strong unions get extremely generous wage agreements without much trouble. Weaker unions have to drag the city into crippling strikes trying to get a good deal.

The Charter puts Muni Railway employees and those in the Craft Unions in special "high pay" categories and leaves the great mass of miscellaneous employees to fend for themselves. That's why the Charter must be changed and that's why we support Proposition "L" on the November ballot.

Proposition "L" would place precise limits around all City pay scales, in most cases 3% above or below what others get for doing the same kind of work. The standard would be based on comparable public and private employment around California.

If passed, nobody's salary would be cut, but raises for some who are now making more than the prescribed limits, would be slowed down. Proposition "L" would also allow the Board of Supervisors to give necessary cost of living increases each year.

We suspect most of you would agree when we say that pay reform is long overdue in San Francisco. Let's show it by voting "yes" on Proposition "L"—the "Fair Pay Amendment"—on November 5th.

EDITORIAL REBUTTAL BY JOSEPH FREITAS, CAMPAIGN COORDINATOR CITIZENS UNITED AGAINST PROP. L

San Francisco has justifiably prided itself as being the most progressive city in the nation in regard to labor-management relations, and collective bargaining is the very keystone of that great tradition. On your ballot this year is Prop. L—a measure that would threaten that hard-won right.

Prop. L will establish a wage freeze for an undetermined period of time for more than 65 per cent of city employees, at a time when they, like everyone else, are suffering the ravages of double-digit inflation.

Even more seriously, Prop. L would repeal San Francisco's recently adopted Employee Relations Ordinance, thereby wiping out all hope of estalbishing meaningful collective bargaining —and true reform. In addition, Prop. L discriminates most viciously against women and low-paid workers by tying their salaries to low and sub-standard wages in the private sector.

The Chamber and other Downtown interests mistakenly believe that, by eliminating collective bargaining, and replacing it with a rigid formula for establishing city employee wage and salary standards, San Francisco will enjoy labor-management harmony. Nothing could be farther from the truth.

This station has expressed concern about strikes by public employees, a concern we all share. But if there ever was a gold-plated invitation for public employees to walk off the job, it is contained in the complicated and punitive charter provisions of Prop. L.

The beginning of true reform lies in the overwhelming rejection of Prop. L at the polls on November 5, and an insistence that the Board of Supervisors face up to its responsibilities and engage in honest collective bargaining with our city employees.

For your own protection, vote NO on Prop. L.

COLUMN ITEMS

There are two kinds of columns. One is a mishmash of news, gossip, trivia, scandal, jokes, and so forth. This kind is usually made up of many unrelated items tied together by the writer's style. The other is an essay or analysis of a particular situation, personality, or issue.

If you are submitting items to the former write them in the style of the columnist. If your favorite columnist never uses items longer than three lines, don't send in three pages, unless it is three pages of three-line items. Even then put the items on separate sheets. If you want to catch the notice of a columnist who fills the whole space with one topic or related topics, it's a good idea to phone and follow up by letter or a visit.

Once the columnist receives a good story from an organization, he or she is generally receptive to others. A potential mayoral candidate seen with a certain political strategist, a celebrity supporting your cause in an unusual way, an anecdote overheard by a prominent labor leader—such stories are all grist for a columnist's mill. But don't overdo it. Pests soon find that the columnist ignores their phone calls.

There is also a golden rule about columnists: If you have more than one in your town—especially if they work for competing papers—*never* give the same item to both. You'll be ignored by both, forever. Also, as much as you may want publicity, it's not a good idea to give stories to a columnist that could be turned into something potentially mean or embarrassing for someone—stories about the District Attorney being seen with a certain blonde in your restaurant, for instance. Eventually, you'll be nailed as the source and you can say goodbye to a lot of friends.

OP-ED

A recent development in the print media is the op-ed page, which is named for its placement *op*posite the *ed*itorial page. Most newspapers with a national reputation have this kind of space. The purpose of the op-ed page is to publish editorial opinions on subjects of the day representing viewpoints other than those of the newspaper.

Op-ed pieces provide one of the few opportunities you will have to present your side exactly as you perceive it, in writing. Like free speech messages, op-ed pieces are time-consuming to write but they are worth it because they are widely read and more credible to the general public than the same information would be as a paid advertisement. In fact, one of the best uses of op-ed pieces is as reprints and clip sheets.

The editorial page and the op-ed page usually have a different editor, just to make things sporting. Op-ed editors, by and large, look for timely subjects, lively writing, and contributions by people who are well known or closely associated with an issue or idea. They tend to be more adventurous in their world view than editorial page editors. They seek to provoke controversy and discussion. Often a good reason to ask for space on the op-ed page is that the paper has come out against your position. Remember that unlike broadcast media, the print media are under no obligation to give equal time or space. Here you must sell your ideas on the basis of general interest and timeliness.

A good way to place an op-ed pieces is to call the editor of the page and suggest your idea or ideas, as well as one or two proposed authors. If the editor finds the subject interesting, ask what length is preferred? When is the deadline? Will they furnish the art or photo, or will you? Will it run on a weekday or on Sunday? Op-ed pages often have fairly strict length regulations, so if the editor tells you to submit a 750-word piece, you can not turn in 1200 words and have it run uncut. The best way to avoid cuts is to follow orders and write to fill the space— exactly. This also goes for the content. If you agree to write an analysis, for example, you cannot submit a tirade or a denunciation.

Try to suggest in op-ed pieces not only what's wrong, but also what the remedy might be. Then try to substantiate what you say from firsthand experience or reliable sources. Since a popular format is to run both sides of a given argument side by side, you should anticipate your opponent's objections, but don't use your space to make them. Use your space to tell *your* story. If people disagree, it's up to them to find the space to rebut your message.

If the subject is difficult, complex, or drawn out, don't assume your reader has followed every twist and turn in the argument. It is always a good idea to begin with a brief review of the topic, and then proceed from there to current developments, your position, what you think ought to happen next, and so on.

If you are talking about a particularly timely subject and are willing to devote the energy to it, there is no reason why you shouldn't think big. Major newspapers and broadcasters are interested in your views. If you have something to say and the credentials to say it, don't forget to write places like the *New York Times* and *Washington Post.* Include a little about your organization and your proposed author along with the story or article idea.

Op-ed pieces include the basic information plus the name of the author and a three-line biography. They also have the word length of the piece, and the date and section where the piece is expected to appear. Start writing on the first page about halfway down. Double space all copy and use wide margins. At the end of each page where there is more copy to come write "(more)," and at the end of the article write "#."

Make sure all pictures are identified. Don't forget to credit the photographer or artist.

THE PLANNING DEPARTMENT IS PLANNING OUR DOOM
BY
ROBERT C. PRITIKIN

The San Francisco Planning Department is singularly responsible for the depletion of middle and low-cost housing in our city. They must be held accountable as the primary factor in ever-spiraling rentals because their restrictive and discriminatory zoning and re-modeling ordinances have prevented the construction and rehabilitation of tens of thousands of new units. They alone must bear the responsibility for the cultural loss to our city of dozens of treasured victorians and the loss in taxes and other revenues to the city in the hundreds of millions of dollars. When the facts become known, it will be a city-wide disgrace.

Thousands of entrepreneurial, creative citizens and thousands more simple homeowners will offer horror stories involving ruinous bureaucratic delays, harassment, vendettas and even some conspiracies for which they have been the victims of this tiny, elitist, insulated staff inside the SF Planning Department.

A highly generalized planning code of enormous ambiguity, endorsed almost casually by a former Board of Supervisors is the bible from which the Planning Dept. staff interprets at its will. Facts will bare out that the SF Planning Dept.—presumably created to serve in the public interest—has amassed such power as to supersede in authority every single department of the City and County of San Francisco including the Police Dept., the Dept. of Public Works, the Mayor's Office, The City Attorney's Office and at least one department of the State of California.

Few of the needless, costly and harassing problems they create ever come up for arbitration before the Planning Commission. The widely publicized crisis into which they have plunged the historic Mansion Hotel (which I created as a mission of love to protect and restore a crumbling monument) is only the tip of the iceberg.

Speak to any of hundreds of small independent building contractors or independent architects and they will recite countless nightmares that they and their clients have been forced to endure. A former SF Cable Car Gripman is on the verge of losing his two unit building into which he put years of effort and tens of thousands of dollars—because of a dispute with the Planning Dept. Indeed, he is a *former* gripman because, according his testimony, the Planning Dept. arranged for his dismissal from his city job, one which he held for years with a perfect record. Two days before he was fired, a City Building Inspector told him if he didn't conform to the Planners wants, he could lose his job.

In another case, a licensed contractor submitted simple plans to the Planning Dept. for the construction of a deck on a middle-priced rental unit. The Planning Dept. informed him it would be months before his application could be reviewed because of their heavy backlog. Sinc ehe is a licensed contractor and designed the deck to code specifications, he knew that approval would be perfunctory. But the landlord had to endure an empty apartment for months, losing perhaps thousands of dollars in rental income—perhaps later trying to make up the loss with increased rents. And during that time the city would lose another apartment rental, further reducing rentor competition and driving up rents even higher.

There are thousands of square blocks within the City and County of San Francisco under the building and remodeling jurisdiction of the Planning Department. Each block could effortlessly provide a number of more middle and low cost rental units—supplied not by city housing funds, but by the investment of dollars of private property owners. The potential is for tens of thousands of new small units. The Planning Dept. won't let them do it.

For instance, the Planners decree density restrictions that favor large backyards where a tiny rear garden unit could otherwise be extended. Some of our city's most charming and inhabitable apartments are those so called "illegal" studio dwellings whose open spaces are garden lightwells or six by twelve foot trellised gardens.

With unrelenting fervor the planners demand "off-street" parking garages for new construction or remodeling a larger home into units. One would think they are more concerned with housing for cars than with housing for people. The valuable limited space with constitutes our tiny San Francisco oasis should be reserved for people first.

LETTER OF INQUIRY

This kind of letter usually outlines an idea or proposal about your project. In the tone you hope the article, interview, or show will take, it tells what you think is important or interesting. It usually suggests a point of view or a conclusion. It also includes a little about the writer or organization if they might not be familiar to the editor or producer.

DATE: November 4, 1980
TO: Leona Wong, KPIX-TV
FROM: Toni Delacorte
RE: *Al Cribari on People Are Talking*

When I first met Al Cribari, his non-nonsense, anti-snob approach to the subject of wine made me feel certain he'd make a perfect regular guest on "People Are Talking" on Channel 5.

While I have heard Cribari described as the "Joe Carcione of wine", I feel he has a lot more graciousness and humor. Perhaps "Wine 101" would be a better description of the way he communicates.

Cribari is the grandson of the man who actually turned the first hoe of soil to start the vineyard which is now the largest in California open to the public. He is capable of talking about virually every aspect of wine—how it's made, how it's marketed, how it's consumed, how to cook with it, how to really enjoy it.

In my estimation, Cribari is a joyful person who truly loves to talk (and is not limited by the subject of wine) and who has the ability to make others feel confortable.

In addition to the information package I have attached containing bio information and several articles written by Cribari and about him, I also have a video tape of a guest appearance he made last year on a Buffalo TV station's noon news.

I sincerely hope you and the producer of People Are Talking will be inviting Al Cribari to KPIX soon. If you are as convinced as I am that he would make a great addition as a regular on the show, I would be happy to discuss program topic ideas in more detail.

Confirmations

Confirm all bookings, appointments, interviews, and the like in writing. Also, confirm in writing any other arrangements you make over the phone.

Carlotta Campbell
KMEL Radio
2300 Stockton St.
San Francisco, CA 94113

Carlotta—

This will confirm that J.P. Phillips will be in the studio to tape a segment for the Berkeley Shakespeare Festival on Monday, June 3 at 11:30 A.M.

I have enclosed the information requested on the Festival's past history and upcoming season, as well as a bio on J.P. Please call me if you need further information or materials.

Thanks again-

Judy Kimsey

Thank-You Notes

Thank-you notes should contain the basic information, plus your thanks, including what you specifically liked about the coverage. A thank-you note is sent to the persons whom you want to thank and, if the job was particularly good, to their boss or bosses. No example is provided. Everyone knows how to say thank-you.

PRESS KIT MATERIAL

The following items are used in the press kit, which is normally handed out at an event at which news coverage will take place. However, some discretion and judgment is required here. You may want to send some of the information with a release ahead of time. After the conference or event, you can make your radio phone-in statements and deliver the press kit to any media representatives who did not attend (see the section on door lists).

Select the appropriate materials for your press kit. It should always include the release and photos. Beyond that, choose wisely. A press kit with all of these items in it is overkill, to say the least:

Fact sheet
Clip sheet
List of contacts
Photos and photo backings
Position paper
Chronology
Biography
Press schedule
Prepared statement

These items are described and examples are given in the following sections.

Fact Sheet

In addition to the basic information, a fact sheet must contain facts and their source. No cheating is allowed.

Indian Facts From Indian Action
1300 Sansome St.
San Francisco 94111   Nov. 15, 1973

Contact: Anson Moran
         Susan Halas

POPULATION	United States	California
Reservation	500,000 (est.)	130,000
Non-reservation	200,000 (est.)	160,000
Total	792,000	290,000

Bay Area Total: 44,000 San Francisco total: 20,000

The "Indian problem" in California is increasingly an urban one.

Employment And Income
* over 40% of all Indians are unemployed (80% on some reservations)
* 50% of Indian families (avg. 5.4 people vs. 2.9 for non-Indian families) earn under $2,000 per year; 75% under $3,000 year.

Education
* 42% of Indian children drop out of school.
* 19% of Indians over 14 have no schooling.
* 60% have less than eighth grade education.

Health
* Average life expectancy for Indians is 47 years.
* Indian mortality rate compared with non-Indian

pneumonia	3.4 times
meningitis	9.4 times
infant	1.4 times (2nd through 12th month)
TB	8 times
liver	4 times
diabetes	3 times
suicide	3 times

Transition To Urban Life
* economic incentive is to leave the reservation
* most find transition to hostile environment difficult.
* once an Indian has left the reservation the Bureau of Indian Affairs disclaims responsibility and no State or Federal agency makes any significant effort to insure that Indians get a reasonable share of assistance targeted for minorities.

Data Source: NY Times Almanac 1972, Region IX American Indian Council (US Govt.)

Clip Sheet

A clip sheet is a reproduction of clippings from a reliable editorial source like a daily paper, a trade paper, or a magazine. In addition to the basic information, a clip sheet should at least identify the source of the clip or clippings and the date and page.

List of Contacts

Reporters are often lazy or pushed for time. You can help them ask the right questions by providing the names, addresses, and phone numbers of the people who have the answers.

If the subject has been covered in some detail in papers outside your immediate area, put the names and phone numbers of those papers on the contact sheet.

INFORMATION SHEET: CONSTANCIO "TINO" DEOCAMPO

Rex Sater, Attorney (707) 542-0734
1212 Collage Ave
Santa Rosa, California 95404

Native American Defense Fund
Tino DeOcampo Committee
2700 Bancroft Way
Berkeley, California
Contact: Susan Reece

Susan Halas, (415) 392-9962
Public Interest Communications
1300 Sansome Street
San Francisco, California 94111

Jewel DeOcampo (707) 691-2583
157 Apt. "A"
Denton Court
Vallejo, California

Previous press coverage available in the morgue of:
Daily Union Democrat, by-line Russell Chandler, Sonora
Cal. (209) 532-7151

Vallejo Times Herald, Vallejo Cal. (707) 644-4121

Modesto Bee, Modesto Cal. (209) 524-4041

Stockton Record, Stockton Cal. (209) 466-2652

SEND DONATIONS TO:
The Constancio (Tino) DeOcampo Legal Defense Fund
Bank of America, Springtown Branch
Account #5-2967
Vallejo, California 94590

Photos and Photo Backings

Photographs should be at least 5 × 7 and preferably 8 × 10. Do not expect them to be returned. Photos should be black and white, especially for print media, but it doesn't hurt to have color photos ready, in case you negotiate to have them appear on a magazine cover. Photos are of two types: vertical (tall and skinny) and horizontal (short and wide). Again, it is nice to give the editor a choice. However, a horizontal photo is used more frequently.

Pictures of one person handing another person a gavel or a trophy or putting a foot on a shovel at a groundbreaking are clichés and to be avoided, as are group shots of the Little Men's Marching and Chowder Society at their weekly Friday lunch meeting. Photo editors like crime, sex, animals, little children, and action shots of all kinds. As for true clichés, a photo really is worth a thousand words.

A photo backing is like a miniature press release. It contains the basic information, plus a caption that identifies the people and objects in the photo from left to right. Photo captions are brief and to the point. Never write on the back of a photo with a ball point pen or pencil. Captions are usually typed on a sheet of paper, and glued or taped to the back of the photo. Don't forget to credit the photographer.

Position Paper

A position paper is usually used when the issue is controversial. The paper should state clearly the organization's stand on the subject, and the reasons behind the position. Political candidates often issue position papers on specific issues as well.

SEVENTY-TWO YEAR OLD GUISEPPE CERVETTO AS CHRISTOPHER COLUMBUS "DISCOVERS" SAN FRANCISCO AS PART OF THE PAGEANTRY CONNECTED WITH THE CELEBRATION OF COLUMBUS DAY. SAILING INTO THE CITY ABOARD THE HARBOR EMPEROR, ONE OF THE RED & WHITE FLEET'S HISTORICAL CRUISE SHIPS, "COLUMBUS" RE-ENACTS THE DISCOVERY OF THE NEW WORLD.

POSITION PAPER
for
NATIONAL WOMENS POLITICAL CAUCUS
ELIJAH TURNER

Equal Rights Amendment

During my civil rights work in the South, I learned two things that I consider important. First, I learned what role women, both black and white, played in the fight for black rights. Historically, women were among the first supporters *and* among the first leaders at a time when womans place was definitely considered to be "in the home".

I also learned that it is not enough to say "I support" or "I endorse". Everyone has got to get out and work and fight for the passage of ERA.

As a member of Oakland's City Council, I will lobby anywhere, at any time, for the passage of ERA. I will honor the boycott against unratified states, and I will be available to members of this caucus whenever I am needed.

Abortion

Women should control their own bodies. It is not my place, nor the place of any other man, to tell a woman she can or cannot have an abortion.

I also want to be sure that abortion does not become a "right of the rich". An unwanted pregnancy or unplanned child can wreak economic havoc in a poor or borderline poor family.

We must see to it that abortion is readily available and affordable to *all* women.

Child Care

We must provide the best child care possible for our children. We need to minimize red tape while maximizing standards.

I would like to see a Citizens Advisory Committee on Child Care, consisting of parents, teachers, and qualified professionals. This committee could help qualified parties to set up centers, and could also weed out many of the problems that we face with the current child care situation.

The early care a child receives determines his or her future. If the care is good, we have a well-balanced, productive citizen. If the care is lacking in any respect, the child may carry permanent scars.

Our children are our future. We must assure that they have the best care possible.

Affirmative Action

If women can bring us into this world, they should certainly help run it.

We need to develop an affirmative action program that will maximize the involvement of women and minorities in the market place. We need to improve the possibilities for advancement and pay increases. The city of Oakland creates 180,000 jobs per year. 100,000 jobs for Oakland residents would wipe out unemployment. In short, we have a job drain in which women and minorities are getting the short end of the stick. Ultimately, the city and the entire country suffer from this discrimination.

We need to "Hire Oakland", and to see to it that women are among the first hired.

Chronology

If an issue is long or complicated people often don't remember the sequence of events. It helps, therefore, if you write it out, keeping the tone factual and giving the source of your information.

NATIVE AMERICAN
DEFENSE   CONTACT: Susan Halas
                                 (415) 824-8091

CHRONOLOGY:

Sept. 9, 1972   Constancio (Tino) DeOcampo, MiWok Indian, age 36 and his wife Jewel and brother William leave Vallejo to attend an all tribes Acorn Festival in Sonora. They are casually invited to a party after the celebration. The party is crowded, (est. 80–100). In course of evening fight breaks out. Everybody runs. Andrew Nelson, white youth, age 20, is shot and dies instantly.

Sept. 9, 1972   Sheriff's Dept. arrests Lionel Meyi.

Sept. 20, 1972   Meyi released for lack of evidence.

Sept. 21, 1972   Tino DeOcampo arrested and charged with first degree murder. Jamestown Justice Court Judge Lillian Snyder sets bail at $150,000.

Oct. 3, 1972   DeOcampo retains Santa Rosa attorney Rex Sater and enters a plea of innocent. Judge Snyder refuses to lower bail in spite of character references from police and city officials in Vallejo.

Oct. 5, 1972   The Tuolumne County Grand Jury refuses
to indict DeOcampo. Dist. Atty. Office issues a statement that charges will not be
dropped and a pre-trial hearing will be held.

Oct. 10 & 11   Preliminary examination held before James-
1972   town Justice Court Judge T. Wesley Os-
borne (sitting in for vacationing Judge Snyder) denies defense motion to drop charges
and also denies motion to produce transcript of grand jury proceedings. Eight witnesses give conflicting testimony. Witness
Ray Bernido testifies drinking 15 beers followed by 10 joints. Witness Michelle Gavi
testifies that she was in the kitchen rolling
joints when she heard the shot and swept
house before police arrived. Quantities of
marijuana, pills and other unidentified,
unanalysed and subsequently missing drugs
found on premises. Murder weapon has not
been found. Prosecution refuses to lower
the charge. Bail lowered by judge to $25,-
000. Case bound over to Superior Court.

Oct. 19, 1972   DeOcampo arraigned in Superior Court,
Tuolumne Co., before Judge Ross Carkeet
who orders new preliminary examinations,
sends case back to Justice Court on grounds
that justice court denied defendant a substantial right to defense by refusing his request for a transcript of grand jury testimony.

Nov. 21, 1972   Superior Court sends case back to Justice
Court. Judge Carkeet quoted as saying,
"This is the first time in my 36 years on the
bench a preliminary hearing has been held
after the grand jury has refused to indict,"
(Sonora Union Dem., Nov. 21, 1972).

Jan. 16, 1973   Justice Court Judge Lillian Snyder finds sufficient evidence after hearing 5 witnesses to send case back to Superior Court.

Jan. 29, 1973   Defense moves again for dismissal on grounds of lack of evidence.

Feb. 15, 1973   Superior Court Judge Ross Carkeet denies motion and sets trial date for June 4 in Sonora Superior Court.

Biography

A biography is helpful if you are having a distinguished guest and don't want to recap his or her accomplishments over and over again. Keep the bio short and to the point. A phone number where the person can be reached is also helpful.

Biography
WILSON RILES JR.

BORN: May 11, 1946 in Flagstaff, Arizona.

EDUCATION: C.K. McClatchy High School, Sacramento

Student Body President
Boy's State Representative

Stanford University, Palo Alto.

Athletic Scholarship
Defensive Halfback for the Cardinals
B.A. in Psychology, 1968.

University of California, Berkeley.

PhD. in Educational Psychology near completion.

FAMILY: Son of Louise and Wilson Riles Sr., State Superintendent of schools. Married Letitia Carter in 1969. They live in Oakland with their two daughters, Elizabeth, who is five, and Vanessa, who is four months.

WORK: Since 1976, Wilson has been Supervisor John George's Administrative Assistant. As Citizen's Advisory Committee Coordinator, Wilson is instrumental in finding solutions to a variety of problems.

Wilson worked in the educational field for two years (1974–1975) first as a math teacher at Hoover Jr. High in Oakland, and then as a program evaluator for Educational Testing Service.

His political career began with his participation in his father's successful campaign for State Superintendent of Schools. From 1970–73, Wilson worked for Weiner & Co., organizing campaigns for Congressmen Pete Stark and Pete McCloskey. In 1972, he managed Congressman Ron Dellum's campaign.

Wilson also spent two years with the Peace Corps in West Africa, and a summer in Harlem with Vista.

Wilson is a member of: California Association of Health Systems Agencies; Northern California Full Employment Coalition; Niagara Democratic Club; N.A.A.C.P.; Congress of Human Needs; Chairman, Executive Advisory Committee to Ron Dellums. The family attends Church of All Faiths in Oakland.

Press Schedule

A press schedule is issued when a series of related events will occur at different times or locations. It is issued to help the media keep track of events and cover the ones that fit their schedule. The whole schedule should fit on one page, and include a thumbnail sketch of what is expected to happen.

Electricity and Gas for People (E&GP)
. . . Turn PG&E around . . .
2831 7th St.
Berkeley, Ca.

Contact: Susan Halas
         Judy Bloom

April 19, 1974

TENTATIVE SCHEDULE OF EVENTS: TUESDAY, APRIL 23, 1974

9:45 A.M.   Secret Public Utilities Commission Meeting, State Building 350 McAllister, Rm. 5039, San Francisco. Dick Revenaugh, reporter for the SF Examiner, recently arrested for protesting PUC secret meeting policy will attempt to once again challenge the closed door meetings. He *may* be joined by other representatives of the press and political world.

12:30 P.M.   March: begins at Bank of America Plaza, California & Kearny Sts. and proceeds past various corporate headquarters to annual

PG&E stockholders meeting, 77 Beale St., SF.

2:00 P.M. (inside)	Electricity and Gas for People delegation, headed by group chairman Mike Miller, will be joined by Democratic gubernatorial candidate Bob Moretti. The delegation, representing 2500 shares of PG&E stock, will take consumer viewpoint to the floor of the stockholders meeting. Moretti has signed a E&GP accountability agreement to oppose the pending $233 million profit rate hike, disclose campaign contributions from utilities, and if elected to appoint consumer advocates to the PUC.
2:00 P.M. (outside)	Rally: The PG&E Octopus—Profit Greed & Exploitation will make his many tentacled debut. Also on hand will be the Golden Calf (an exact replica of the one denounced by Moses). The first annual Golden Calf Award symbolizing "private gain at the public expense" has been presented to PG&E Chairman Shermer Sibley.

A MINIMUM OF 500 people are expected to participate in the inside and outside actions of Electricity & Gas for People

Prepared Statement

In a prepared statement basic information should appear, plus the name of the speaker, affiliation, age, and occupation. A contact phone for the speaker is also useful.

STATEMENT BY JOAN PASSALACQUA REGARDING THE BROADCAST LICENSE RENEWAL BILL

The Broadcast License Renewal Bill is an attempt by the industry to keep groups like those represented here today from filing petitions to deny and from pressuring local broadcasters to respond to their communities and audience.

The public is up against great odds, for our representatives in Congress must rely on the broadcasting industry for access to the people. And so, Senators and Congresspeople, who have in the past voted against "special interest" legislation have supported this bill which was opposed by over 90 community groups in recent testimony before the Senate with the only supporters being people who represented the broadcasting industry.

But regardless of what happens in Congress, community groups striving for a more responsive media are here to stay.

Three years ago, at the last license renewal in California, there were more petitions to deny filed than ever before, and today more petitions will be filed against local broadcasters than in 1971. We are growing, more people are joining and new groups are forming. and so until local broadcasters respond to the needs, interests and problems of all groups in the community, petitions to deny will continue to be filed.

INTERNAL ORGANIZATIONAL MATERIALS

The third grouping of press materials consists of items for internal organizational use. They make keeping track of publicity efforts easier.

Call Sheet

Call sheets are for internal use; they help you keep track of the people you need to alert regarding scheduled news events. Take the sheet with you to the event. Give it to your speakers or to the people you have set up for interviews. Don't forget to include—in case of an emergency—a number for your own organization and for the person who set up the events and bookings.

A call sheet is a list of the reporters you have contacted for an event. It includes *phone numbers,* and usually, the name of the newspaper or station.

You should also add important names and phone numbers of people who are involved in the project that members of the press might want to speak with.

Carry this list with you, and keep a copy in the office.

Press List

A press list is invaluable. It is a listing of all contacts, complete with the name of the publication or station and the address. Put each on contact labels to make press mailings easier. The same organization may have several press lists, depending on how it functions and why. For example, a consumer group may have a press list for calendar and PSA announcements, and another for city desk and assignment editors.

Do not mail to a name. Mail to "News Assignment Editor" or City Desk, or Community Calendar. Media people tend to move around a lot, and last week's assignment editor at Channel 2 may be this week's public service director at Channel 3.

By mailing to to the title, your release will be opened by the appropriate person.

Entertainment Editor
INDEPENDENT
&GAZETTE
2043 Allston Way
Berkeley, CA 94704

Entertainment Editor
San Francisco Chronicle
901 Mission Street
San Francisco, CA 94103

Entertainment Editor
San Francisco Examiner
110 Fifth Street
San Francisco, CA 94103

Entertainment Editor
CONCORD
TRANSCRIPT
1741 Clayton Road
Concord, CA 94522

Entertainment Editor
PENINSULA
HERALD
Box 271
Monterey, CA 93940

Entertainment Editor
SAN JOSE
MERCURY NEWS
750 Ridder Park Drive
San Jose, CA 95190

Entertainment Editor
OAKLAND
TRIBUNE
409 13th Street
Oakland, CA 94612

Entertainment Editor
SAN MATEO TIMES
1080 S. Amphlett
San Mateo, CA 94402

Entertainment Editor
PENINSULA
TIMES-TRIBUNE
Box 300
Palo Alto, CA 94302

Entertainment Editor
HAYWARD DAILY
REVIEW
Box 5050
Hayward, CA 93230

Entertainment Editor
KRON TV NEWS
1001 Van Ness Blvd.
San Francisco, CA 94109

Entertainment Editor
KGO-TV NEWS
277 Golden Gate Ave.
San Francisco, CA 94102

Assignment Desk
KSBW TV NEWS
238 John Street
Salinas, CA 93901

Producer: David Cox Show
KSBW TV
238 John Street
Salinas, CA 93901

Lilian Rojas Show
KMST-TV
46 Garden Court
Monterey, CA 93940

Assignment Desk
KMST
46 Garden Court
Monterey, CA 94940

Assignment Desk
KPIX TV NEWS
855 Battery Street
San Francisco, CA 94111

Entertainment Editor
SAN FRANCISCO
PROGRESS
851 Howard Street
San Francisco, CA 94103

Food Editor
SAN FRANCISCO
PROGRESS
851 Howard Street
San Francisco, CA 94103

Entertainment Erutor
SAN RAFAEL
INDEPENDENT
JOURNAL
P.O. Box 330
San Rafael, CA 94902

Food Editor
SAN RAFAEL
INDENPENDENT
JOURNAL
P.O. Box 330
San Rafael, CA 94902

Booking Schedule

A booking schedule is an important document for internal use. It tells day by day and hour by hour who went where, with whom, and for how long. It also tells when the resulting story will run and whether it's confirmed or pending.

One person should do all the booking from one place. Do not change bookers in midstream. If they call to talk to Helen, who set up the interview, they won't like it if it is Allen's department today and Joe's department tomorrow. All contacts are personal. That is, once you have finally found your way through the switchboard maze into the right departments, into the person in charge, to a reporter, and into print or on the air, those contacts are *your* contacts. You may help others if you like, but you don't have to. Keep your files confidential.

BOOKING SCHEDULE:

Tues, Oct. 1
1:30 Willie Hearst, Examiner Other Voices, Will run Sun.
Oct. 6 or Sun Oct 12. About 2 P.M.

Wed. Oct. 2
9:30 A.M. Maxine with Tom Watson, editor of SF Progress.
10 A.M. Dennise at KYA, 1 Nob Hill, Mason at Pine, will start 3 times a day for a week.

Thurs., Oct. 3
KSAN 10:30 A.M. Denice and Maxine with Denise Bordett
5:30 tape with Iris Grayson KFRC, 415 Bush, free speech bring script.

Mon., Oct. 7
10 A.M. KRON, 55 seconds, Nancy with Bob Heald, 5 times in one week.
4 P.M. Dick Pearche, Examiner.

Tues, Oct. 8
10 A.M. Bonnie KABC, free speech, Harry Websert, 4
times.

Wed. Oct 9
10 A.M. K101 radio with Maxine, Jack Anderson, tape to
air sunday.
10 A.M. KNBR group of 5 with moderator, for half hour,
will air Sunday.

Door List

Take the call sheet for a scheduled news event to the event.
As reporters arrive, check them off the list. Or, keep a list and
compare it to the call sheet later. Anyone who did not cover the
event should have a press kit hand-delivered. No example. You
know how to make a list.

Press Coverage Report

A press coverage report sheet contains the basic information
plus a summary of all the coverage you have received on a given
subject or event. The summary can be done either by date or
arranged according to media (print, television, radio). Attach
copies of print clips and broadcast scripts.

This is the only evidence you have that your media campaign
is working. Make sure you evaluate it. Find out what works for
you.

Final Report: Public Relations Thurs. Oct. 17, 1974
Susan Halas
690 Arkansas St.
San Francisco 94107

FREE SPEECH MESSAGES (see booking sheet)
KRON-TV, Nancy Musser, runs onces a day for five days
KABL radio, Bonnie Lum, runs twice a day A.M. & P.M.
Oct. 9—15
KFRC, Iris Grayson, (4 times a day Oct. 12 & 13)
KTVU-TV, Charlene Wiggins (schedule not yet set)
KYA radio, Denise D'Anne, (once a day for a month
between 12–3P.M.)

RADIO & TV:
KNBR—group session, half hour, aired Sun., Oct. 13
K101—group session, hour, aired Sun., Oct. 13
KSFO—group of three, will air prime time (P.M. drive)
after election
KGO TV—Jenkins, Call Out, 30 min, will air Sun, Oct. 20
KGO TV—Jenkins debates Feinstein, will air Mon. Oct.
28 7:30–8:30 A.M.
KCBS AM—Jenkins interview, air before election 10 min
max.
KCBS FM—Jenkins interview, aired no date available, 10
min max.
KSAN radio—Jenkins interview, aired no date available,
5 min max.
KPIX-TV—Jenkins, The Noon News, 5 min, will air be-
fore election

RESULTS OF CITY HALL SWITCHBOARD OPERA-
TORS PRESS CONFERENCE
TUES. OCT. 8, 1974
SF Chronicle, (page 16, Oct. 9) 8 col. inches
SF Examiner, (page 2, Oct. 8) 11 col inches

KGO TV early and late news
KPIX TV early and late news
KRON TV 5:30, 6:30 and 11P.M.
KGO radio P.M. news at least once
KDIA radio 1:20, 3:30 and possibly the late P.M. news
KCBS radio A.M. and P.M. drive time
Also present at press conference: Bay Guardian, Sun Reporter
KYA, KPFA. Statements given on phone to: KFRC,KNBR,K101,KSFO

EDITORIALS
SF Chronicle/Examiner, Jenkins on Op-Ed page, Sun. Oct. 13, 36col inch
Materials sent requesting endorsement or rebuttal to: KRON TV,
KPIX-TV, KTVU-TV, KGO-TV, KNBR radio, KCBS-A.M. radio.
KPIX editorialized a YES vote. Rebuttal taped and aired (Joe
Freitas Jr.) Four times, noon and 7P.M. on two consecutive days.
KRON-TV will probably take our editorial rebuttal written by
a clerk typist member Gloria Hunter. Pending.
ALL OTHER EDITORIAL MATERIAL SHOULD BE CLEARED THROUGH:
Susi Holland, Weiner & Co. 986-5545

Other:
Herb Caen, October 2

3
Why, When, Where, and How: The Feature—Soft News

Definition and Overview: A Personal Appearance

The preceding chapters have discussed the who and what of public relations. This chapter and the next describe the why, when, where, and how for dealing with both feature and hard news.

WHY

The personal appearance tour (PA) is the key to feature news. If your idea, issue, personality, or organization is new, complicated, or controversial, the best way to make the public aware of it is through the PA. A PA means sending a person, or variety of people, on the rounds from station to station or paper to paper and interviewing with news, feature editorial, and public affairs departments.

WHEN

Because fast-breaking news isn't involved, most PA materials can be taped or written well ahead of time. If material is pegged to a date—for example, a benefit on March 6 for battered children—begin bookings with talk shows and feature editors well in advance. Best results can be expected if the shows begin airing about a week and a half before the event. Much earlier, and people forget. Much later, and they've made other plans.

WHERE

Usually, television and radio interviews take place in the studio of the station, while a print reporter will normally come to the scene. Free speech messages must be recorded in the studio. PSA's can either be recorded in the studio or taped elsewhere and mailed in. If the latter course is followed, be sure to work with professional quality tape. One time a group prepared a television PSA for educational purposes. Unfortunately, they did not bother to check with the local stations for their requirements, and recorded the spot on 1-inch tape. The stations all required 2-inch tape, and by the time an expensive process had jumped the tape to 2 inches, the quality was so bad that the spot couldn't be run. So check all technical matters, getting your information directly from those who know. The public affairs director is usually the best source. If he or she can't be reached, try someone in traffic or production.

Most metropolitan areas have an abundance of media outlets, but not all the issues or organizations you'll be working with will be city-oriented. Often matters of vital public interest take place in, or concern, rural areas. Witness the debate on strip mines, the farm labor union question, and the save the wilderness movement. All of these are basically rural concerns that have made contact with urban media. How did they do it? How can you do it?

One way is to issue an invitation to a reporter or writer to come up to the appropriate neck of the woods and look around. Send a letter with the background. If the story is really good, pick your outlet—better one story in the *Washington Post* than a series in the *Podunk Sun.* Write letters, make phone calls, send any local clips that will help an editor understand the situation.

Unless you have a really hot event like the Wounded Knee uprising or the Alaska pipeline, it takes time to establish contact with a national source. Start as far in advance as possible and do not be discouraged if it seems to take forever.

Another good way to get coverage is to work with journalism students who have a professional interest in investigative reporting. They may be able to get your story into print. It is permissible to furnish them a place to stay and something to eat, but it is not permissible to write or edit their stories.

Almost no place is so remote that there isn't a phone somewhere. And where there's a phone, there's a possibility of getting on radio news. Contact the news director of radio stations in the nearest metropolitan area, and call in stories daily or even hourly. This can sometimes pique the interest of the big city press, and the results are often worth the phone bill.

If you can, bring your most important spokespeople to the city to talk to the news media in person. Send one person in advance to do the scheduling and booking so you don't waste time while in town. Country people have a passion for late night talk radio and call-in shows. Be sure to book programs on stations with strong signals so you can be heard back in the outlying area where the story is happening.

Once in a blue moon you may be able to convince a TV producer that it's really worth the expense to send a crew to a rural area, especially if the subject is visually dramatic. (It is too expensive for most groups to shoot their own footage—political campaigns are about the only ones who can afford to do so.) A low-cost version of the same event is 35 mm color slides accompanied by a short script. Remember, TV news and feature stories tend to run well under 2 minutes, so keep it short.

HOW

The first thing required for a PA is at least one live, warm body, whose time is completely at your disposal. This person should have a gift of gab, an even temper, a pleasing voice, and a very thorough understanding of the subject. Since this he or she represents your cause or organization, select carefully. Many times, the president or founder of an organizations feels that he or she is the person who should make all public appearances. This is *not* necessarily true. The president, for example, may be knowledgeable, but if she makes a bad first impression or tends to lose her temper, go with someone else.

Booking a PA is like going shopping—you make a list of what you want and compare it to what's available. Then get on the telephone and contact everyone who schedules the space or time desired. Various editors and producers will react differently to your requests. Don't push those who aren't interested. Go on and find someone else who is.

Next, sit down with the list of "interesteds" and compose a letter of inquiry (a request to have a guest appear). Write the letter as far in advance as possible. After talking to a number of producers or editors, you will have a better idea of how you can sell your spokesperson. Writing is easier after you know what people want. Choose whatever other materials are appropriate and enclose them with the letter of inquiry. Be sure that a biography and history or background information is included.

It is important to look at just what kind of angle interests an editor. If it seems as though the editor is looking to be critical or to sensationalize the subject, turn down the coverage. By the same token, people on the inside of an organization don't always see what's most interesting about themselves. The general membership may find it impressive that the block club represents 82 families and just got a new zoning regulation passed. The editor may think that's ok, but what he's really interested in is the 16-year-old whiz kid who is serving as treasurer. The rule is: Put what's interesting up front, even if it isn't the main point.

When talking with an editor, start from the interesting point and broaden out into more general ideas, causes, reforms, gripes, or suggestions. Be able to support concepts with specific for-instances from reliable sources or firsthand experience. Because not every editor is interested in the same angle, the press materials sent to each should vary. Keep good notes on who has been called and what their interests are, and select back-up materials accordingly.

After the material has been sent, about half the people will call back expressing an interest, and wanting to schedule an interview. The other half will have to be persuaded. This takes time and something to talk about. It also takes subtle pressure. Nobody has to know this but you. While perusing an empty schedule, say "Let me see now, I think maybe I can squeeze you in early Monday morning or late Tuesday afternoon." Of course, these times are chosen out of thin air, since the guest is available continuously for the next 15 years. But, by making it sound as if the editor has to decide now, he or she usually will. Often in deciding between Monday and Tuesday the editor forgets that he originally intended to say no. Send a confirmation when you have agreed on a date and time.

Keep an accurate record in your booking schedule of what is happening. Is the show taped or live? Is it five minutes or half an hour? In a good or bad time slot?

When scheduling, do not book time so tightly that if interview one runs long the guest will be late to interview two. If being late is unavoidable, call. (Send everybody out with a list that has the necessary phone numbers on it just in case.) However, it's better to make the schedule flexible than to be late.

Only book times that can be filled with interesting information. Nobody can fill an hour alone: That's why Johnny Carson has more than one guest. Monologues are a tune-out. Better two minutes on prime time than an hour on the graveyard shift. The obvious virtue of a PA is that, although bookings occur simultaneously, interviews run at different times. The effect sticks around. Keep clips, and don't forget to thank the people who did well by you.

INTERVIEWS

The interview is the staple of the PA. One of the best interviews ever was Bernadette Devlin right after her election to the Parliament of England. Her command of the language was astounding. She talked for days and never said the same thing twice. Listening to her you'd think Derry, Ireland, was the red hot center of the universe.

Reporters prefer to interview well-informed, articulate people with a genuine interest in a given subject. They prefer a relaxed informal atmosphere to a highly structured framework. They prefer to interview people who treat them like human beings and not as enemies or dopes.

Interviews are a give-and-take situation. It helps to arrive on time, be prepared, and bring photos. If your subject is controversial, it is useful if you can remain rational. As in all situations it's best to tell the truth in a colorful quotable manner. Don't mouth clichés. Further, a good guest doesn't stay forever or call back a million times. A good guest is tolerant of minor error and doesn't make a federal case over the shading of a word.

One way to avoid being misquoted is to ask for approval on quotes. No reporter should, or has any obligation to, show you a story before it goes to press. But a writer may agree to give you approval on quotes, which basically means that before anything is run, you'll hear the words that are specifically attributed to you. This favor is rarely extended, however, so it is better to watch what you say than to be angry when half-baked remarks appear in print.

Don't be petty. If a story reports that there were 300 people present when the writer visited the school lunch program, don't get up in arms if there were really 320.

Expect a reporter to be interested in setting the scene—how the guest speaks, what he or she wears. If the guest arrives in a silver jumpsuit and an afro wig, walking a duck on a leash, you can expect that to be part of the story, or worse, the focal point of the story. The best advice is not to allow guests to get into situations where they might be derailed; that is, make the gabby husband or the three-year-old daughter stay home if their company is distracting.

TALK RADIO

Talk radio, a format where a host interviews a guest and then opens phone lines to callers, is perhaps the most participatory form of media we have today. There is a wide audience, not just for a particular host or show, but for the format itself. Whenever possible, schedule people for talk radio, talk radio, and more talk radio.

Almost always the host you hear on the air has some say about the guest that will appear, but often the producer of the show has the major responsibility for guests. Therefore, it is a good idea to make the initial approach to the producer, rather than to the host. A call followed by a letter is standard practice. If you make a booking, send a confirmation.

If you do book a guest for a call-in talk show, make sure someone listens to the show at least once ahead of time. Be sure the guest is briefed on what might be expected from the show's host and on the kind of people who call in. If possible have someone from your organization or at least someone sympathetic phone in with something complimentary or positive. Practice the off-the-wall question, the hostile caller, and the caller who has you mixed up with someone else. The speaker shouldn't become impatient or angry. Have a few funny anecdotes in mind to use as transitions from subjects you don't want to talk about to subjects you do.

SPEAKER'S BUREAU

A speaker's bureau, set up by an organization, can be an important tool for community outreach, and can be used by every type of organization imaginable. Political candidates need back-up speakers when they cannot appear personally; any issue, cause, or organization needs people who can go out and explain why they are doing what they do, why they need money, and any other number of whys; and businesses may find themselves in the position of having to explain to local neighborhood organizations why a proposed expansion will help rather than hurt the community.

Ideally, an organization should have two or more speakers available. These people should be chosen for their ability to speak coherently and clearly, especially if the subject under discussion is complicated. They should also present a good public image—no dirty jeans and cowboy boots unless the local rodeo is the issue.

The publicist, working with the speakers, should develop ahead of time a general speech outline to be followed on most occasions, as well as answers to particularly rough questions. Next, the publicist should do a little research on the group to be addressed and work to relate his or her subject to a specific issue that affects that group. Pass the information to the speaker. Remember, the members of Local 20 want to know how the issue or organization affects them, not what the ultimate effects on senior citizens will be.

There is another good reason for checking out a group requesting one of your speakers. The group might very well not agree with what you are saying. The purpose of speaker's bureaus is to explain and win converts. Therefore, speakers should ideally go where there is a possibility of winning such converts. When there is no such possibility, then sending a speaker is a waste of time and should be avoided. Speakers will also be sent to groups agreeing with you. In this case, sending a representative will help keep goodwill alive and keep people posted on the latest developments.

Initially, the publicist should call around to let people know that a speaker's bureau has been established. Send new speakers to sympathetic organizations at first. It's easier to remedy mistakes with those who support you than with those who think you're nuts and incompetent anyway. Save the hardened veterans for hostile territory.

After you have confirmed with the speaker that he or she can attend on the requested date, confirm the appearance in writing, sending a carbon copy to the speaker, together with pertinent information about the group he or she will speak to.

4

WHY, WHEN, WHERE AND HOW: THE SCHEDULED PRESS EVENT —HARD NEWS

A scheduled news event or press conference can cause even hardened publicists to consider resigning—if they don't die of simple heart attack first. Something always goes awry. Snappy assignment editors hurt your feelings. The main speaker develops an accute attack of nerves and begins to stutter. The photos for the press kit run dangerously late. And, underlying all of these superficial horrors is the real biggie—what if you arrange a press conference and nobody comes!

Know right now that it can happen. Suppose, for example, that 40 minutes before your press conference, a major story broke. Your local bar—and bars in every city where press conferences had been scheduled—would soon be full of weepy, miffed, and tipsy PR people. So, it can happen. But with careful planning and follow-through, it isn't likely. (After all, how many major stories are likely to break just before your press conference?) First, however, you have to know when you have news.

PLANNING A PRESS CONFERENCE

There are several hundred definitions of news, none very helpful. Unfortunately, one really does need the proverbial "nose for news." You can have every tool known to publicists to help you carry out a successful scheduled news event, but if instinct doesn't help you determine what, in fact, is news, its all for naught. To paraphrase a saying in journalism: "Every reporter knows when they have missed a story. The trick is to catch a story." Likewise for the publicist.

In public relations, developing a plan is the most important part. Once you've figured out what you want to do, almost anybody can make the phone calls, or write a release, or take the mail to the post office. But some people have a knack for coming up with good ideas or anticipating bad side effects. For that reason it is especially important to get together as a group and talk things over in advance. It is much easier to plan activities that will result in good media coverage than it is to remedy bad press. If plans are made without considering press requirements, the news event may well have no public impact because no editor will assign a reporter to cover it.

In the planning stages good advice is to think about what will be the most visual. Remember that the best time to get coverage is on weekdays rather than weekends, and in the mornings rather than the afternoons. Just as it is not a good idea to make plans independent of how they will look in print or sound on the air, neither is it a good idea to become a press release revolutionary and make plans exclusively for their media value.

After presenting the where and when of a hard news press conference, the why and how will be examined, along with a day-by-day planning method that should spell success.

WHERE?

"Where" can be either indoors or outdoors, but make sure it is a location that is easy for the press to find. It also helps if it is in a place familiar to them, such as the steps of City Hall or a downtown hotel meeting room. But the most important thing to consider is how the location will look visually. A clean, cheerful office or a nice conference room will reflect a positive visual image—dark basement rooms and busy street corners do not. Be sure too, that the space for the event is large enough to hold your people, the press, and their cameras. If the speakers are seated, the electronic media will appreciate a place to prop their microphones. This avoids having ten reporters with tired arms standing in front of the TV cameras and blocking the view of the print photographers. Although, in these days of mini-cams, life is much easier for the PR person, who no longer has to worry about electric outlets or how far camera cords will reach, factors such as location and space must still be considered.

Make sure that the setting is appropriate. I was traveling with a political candidate for a state office in California when I ran into a most unfortunate setting. We had flown into San Diego, and the advance man in that city was new to campaigning. He had called a major hotel in town, and booked a press room that the management assured him had been used by "many political candidates' in the past. Unfortunately, our young Turk hadn't bothered to check things out in person.

When the press advance crew arrived, the first thing we confronted was a picket line in front of the hotel. If you want to kill off a Democratic candidate in record time, just get him on film crossing a picket line. We left one of our number dealing with that little problem while the rest of us went in to check out the room.

It was a disaster. There was red flocked wallpaper, pink marble cocktail tables, and gilt Louis-the-something-or-other chairs upholstered in red velvet. It looked as if our candidate were getting ready to proclaim himself emperor of All he Surveyed rather than announcing his candidacy for Attorney General.

To add insult to injury, the candidate's table had been set up in front of a floor-length, gilt-edged mirror. The only camera angle possible ensured that not only would the public be made aware of our candidate's smiling face, but also of his backside, the cameras filming him, and whatever lurid affair might be going on in the hall.

Since no other room was available, the press advance man and I rolled up our sleeves, and amidst the shrieks of the hotel management proceeded to arrange King Louis's furniture in a more politically appropriate manner. We survived the press conference by the grace of God.

Also, don't begin planning too many outdoor events. Don't plan them during the rainy season, for example, unless rain is an integral part of your campaign. And don't expect the press to embark on a 3-mile hike. The press will go a long way for a good story, but don't push your luck. The ideal outdoor location is one that is easy to get to via main roads, and has sufficient parking accommodations. If the location is difficult, put up signs, or better yet, have people out directing the press.

WHEN?

For maximum exposure a scheduled news event should take place before 11 A.M. on any Tuesday, Wednesday or Thursday. The later in the day you schedule, the more chance you take that something unscheduled (a fire, murder, scandal, etc.) will break and take all available press away from you. Also, the later in the day you schedule, the more chance there is that crews and reporters will be running behind their schedules and will bump you because something ran longer than expected. Further, the later the event, the harder it is for TV news to film, process, edit, and script the story by the evening deadline. It is not impossible to get coverage for other days and times, just harder.

Community organizations often prefer weekends and evenings for scheduled news events because those are the times they can get maximum participation. However, it is often difficult to get coverage for those times because papers and stations have smaller staffs then. If you plan to schedule in these times, start notification earlier, and try to get definite commitments. Often the weekend is assigned by a different editor than the weekdays, so make sure that the notification and follow-up go to the right person.

Remember that almost everywhere all sections of the Sunday paper are printed earlier in the week. The only exception to this is generally the first section, which contains late Saturday news that is printed on Saturday night.

Other less favorable times to hold a scheduled news event are Monday morning and Friday afternoon. Monday is bad because it creates the greatest opportunity for the confusion and error that comes with the start of the new week. As for Friday, just suppose the press conference is scheduled for 3 P.M. Friday afternoon. The deadlines for the afternoon paper and the early evening TV news have already been missed. If television covers the conference at all, it will appear on the late Friday night news, when most of America is out partying.

Saturday's paper has an average circulation drop of 30 to 50 percent compared with weekdays, and on Saturday morning there is hardly any news at all.

A further time consideration is necessary for the West Coast publicist. Remember that what is 9 A.M. in New York is 6 A.M. in Los Angeles and 3 A.M. in Honolulu. If a really big story is in the making, schedule the West Coast conference early in the morning, on the off chance that it will make it back to New York for the evening news. Or, if budget permits, consider flying back to New York or Washington D.C. and holding the event there, then flying back home and holding the same event. This has another advantage, too, since the media is universally regards anything from out of town as "better." So, the event is better if it has been somewhere else first. Or, if out-of-town moguls, dignitaries, and grand wizards can be imported to back up the hometown position, so much the better.

West Coast stories suffer another editorial prejudice: At least half the things that happen in the West are passed off in the East as not of general interest because they "can happen only in California." What these East Coast editors seem to forget is that a number of movements, trends, and situations that have dominated not only national but also world news, have originated in California. And, a number of other Western states also have things to offer the country.

When you pick a date and time it is essential to get some advance idea of what or who might be scheduled at the same time. One good way to find out is to phone the Associated Press (AP) or the United Press International (UPI). These two international news-gathering organizations each keep a list of scheduled events that they send out at regular intervals during the day by teletype to their clients. You may call them up and ask them to check the file for the time and date you have in mind. Usually they are cooperative about this, but if you get a no, try calling back at a less busy time.

If there is no AP or UPI in your area call the city desk of the leading paper. Obviously, if you find out a week in advance that the Secretary of State is going to be visiting and has the same time and date in mind for his press conference

NEWS EVENT

A scheduled news event usually takes quite a lot of planning, but it is one of the best ways to bring the media together in one place to call attention to a specific situation. A press conference is the most common type of scheduled news event.

Press conferences are good for news that is too important to give out a little at a time or that is pegged to a certain date. A press conference is usually a controlled event. The publicist calls it; the publicist steers it. The publicist decides which questions are going to be answered and when it is going to be over.

When a group takes action and invites the press, another kind of scheduled news event occurs, but this is one whose outcome can be unpredictable. While press conferences are usually called for the specific purpose of briefing the media, group actions usually have some larger goal to which good media coverage is a useful adjunct. It is often difficult to pay proper attention to the press while confronting public officials, or when involved in trying situations with those who hold different views, but it must be done.

Further, even though hundreds of people may see the event with their own eyes at a meeting or rally, it's all wasted on the people at home unless you spend a few minutes interpreting the actions for the cameras and reporters. If what is being done isn't explained clearly and concisely, the media may put a very different slant on the event than the one its sponsors had in mind.

If the press is being taken to or through an action, assemble them at some common starting point and brief them on what to expect. Just because the organization has been hot on the trail of someone for months doesn't mean that everybody else has ever heard of him. So don't call him "Old So and So" and leave it at that. Identify him as "Old So and So, a slum landlord who refuses to bring his building up to code," or "Old So and So, an employer who discriminates against handicapped workers."

By the same token, if you introduce a new business by holding an on-site press conference, be sure to provide a history and background of how it came into existence. Identify the principals. And make sure that you have been through the tour several times yourself before you haul the press along.

If the press arrives unnoticed, and the publicist is either unaware they are there or unprepared to speak with them, be prepared to have your conduct noted in the story.

In planning an action, recheck what might go wrong with the same thoroughness that you check what you hope will happen. If you want to illustrate wide popular support for a proposal at a public meeting, be sure that the time the speaker speaks coincides with the time the press is to be there. Or, if your group is going onto the floor of a stockholder's meeting with a protest, will your people get seats, or will the company pack the hall and let you watch the whole proceedings by closed circuit TV?

In a touchy situation, the best strategy is to get older women up front and make sure the press is with them. Women in the grandmother age bracket make the best points, look the best on camera, sound credible to everyone, and love the attention. This is not to say bad things will always happen, but it emphasizes the need to be prepared and to have alternative plans ready if they do.

Group actions that are press conferences are particularly tricky, and must be planned with care and intelligence. One particularly bad press conference was held by a group of citizens who wanted to express their outrage at the takeover of the Chilean government in 1973 by a military junta. What was wrong with the press conference was:

1. It came months after the actual event. 2. There was only one person present who actually came from Chile and he was scheduled to speak last. 3. No Americans of Chilean ancestry or with family currently in the country were on the speakers' list. 4. The people sponsoring the event were using identifications like "former school board member." Unless you can identify yourself as a former U.S. Supreme Court Justice, just stick to name, organization, and occupation. A school board member (former) has no bearing on moral outrage (delayed).

The conference proved to be an embarrassing event because, though the media was there in force, nobody present could actually shed light on what was going on in Chile. There was merely a nervous group of locals standing up and saying, very much after the fact, "Nasty, nasty, wicked, wicked." That's an editorial opinion, that's not news.

Some time later another group attempted a boycott of Chilean ships in San Francisco harbor, an action that couched a moral judgment within the framework of news: If we don't like their politics abroad, we won't let them unload their goods here. Much more to the point.

Another kind of scheduled event requires media cooperation. If you plan a surprise visit to the director's meeting of the biggest bank in the area, it will not be a surprise if you notify every news desk in town, but it will not be covered at all if you don't notify somebody. This is where leaks are useful. A leak is a selective notification, usually verbal, to trusted reporters. You trade inside information on a good story for their promise to keep the information confidential until you want it released. Ask for an immediate yes or no on coverage, so if one source doesn't want it another can be found that does.

By nature, the leak is exclusive . . . offer the story to one print media outlet and one electronic outlet. If every major newspaper and TV station in town is notified, count on getting into trouble. The reason your chosen media don't release the scoop before the event itself is because they are the only source carrying the story. If it is given to everyone, a mad scramble to see who can break first will ensue, and the real impact may be lost in the shuffle. So remember, *leak* and exclusive are synonymous, and they mean iust what they say.

Sometimes you can get action by *threatening* to hold a press conference. You don't *want* to have a press conference at the Police Department's HQ because someday you will need a parade permit, parking clearance, a block closed for a party or some other consideration. Obviously, nobody wants to be on the bad side of the local police.

But if there are problems with the boys in blue, the media person and another representative of the organization may go to them and say, "It pains us that such and such has happened. We are sure there is a misunderstanding or possibly the papers have just been mislaid. It would be a pity to blow this thing up all out of proportion by holding a press conference. We, personally would prefer to get this matter settled quickly and quietly. However, we are not completely our own boss and besides [as they have probably heard] there are some hot heads in the organization. If this isn't cleared up soon [like tomorrow or the day after], we don't know if we can hold our people."

If satisfaction isn't forthcoming within 48 hours, call back and say, "It looks like we'll be going ahead with our press conference on Monday. Who's going to give the statement for your side?" This puts the opposition at a disadvantage. If they do speak it will acknowledge that the situation is serious enough to require a rebuttal. If they don't speak, make the point that they were offered time and refused.

In my experience, things don't go this far. When the chief starts thinking about what the department is going to say and how it will look and sound, he usually finds a way to keep the whole subject out of the public eye.

Do not bluff. Don't ever try this unless you mean to go through with it if they don't come around.

SCHEDULING AN EVENT: A SUMMARY

If you are considering having a press conference or news event, here's an easy timetable:

WEDNESDAY: Plan date, time, place, action, speakers; delegate authority; plan staffing and security; inform clipping service. Check for conflict on time or date.

THURSDAY: Write/clear/revise materials announcing the event and the collateral material that will be passed out to the press on the day of the event.

FRIDAY: Finish writing the materials. Compile press list. Xerox appropriate number of copies. Mail from the main post office. Mail one to yourself.

MONDAY: Check the room or location. Rehearse with participants. Call the press list to make sure the release has been received and is correctly filed.

TUESDAY: Have other friends of the organization make coordinated phone calls. Make sure you have a roll of dimes and nickels and somebody to work the door the next day.

WEDNESDAY: On the day of the press conference make early morning calls to the press list. Work the door. Check security. Start and end on time. Go back to your contact phone number and write your radio follow-up statement. Phone it in to papers and stations that were not present at the event. If there are any subsequent developments phone them in to reporters who attended the event. Monitor evening coverage.

THURSDAY: Monitor morning coverage. Assess results. Reproduce clips. Write or call thank-yous as appropriate.

Let's go over this schedule in more detail.

WEDNESDAY: PLANNING

The publicist's job as contact is to get the press to the organization, or the organization to the press, with correct information in a form that is easy to understand. Ideally, this means coming up with a catchy story with good visuals. It is the job of the organization, business, and the researchers to keep the media contact well informed and up to date.

Getting ready for a big press conference is likely to be hectic. There's a lot going on, mostly in the head of one person. Although it is difficult to split up functions such as scheduling, jobs such as doing follow-up or research, making phone calls, monitoring, or writing material may be delegated to various members. Remember, however, the more you split the functions the slower things move.

The person who is going to make most of the media contacts should not have numerous other duties during the week preceding the event, because he or she is going to be busy at the phone or typewriter. It is important that this person be easily accessible to the press and sufficiently well informed to answer both routine and more complex questions. If you don't know the answer to a question say, "I don't know, but I'll get back to you. How soon do you need it?" Always return calls promptly.

Who's It For?

When planning an event, the first thing to decide is who's it for? Is it for the public? Select customers? The network? Before calling in the press, decide whether the press will help or aggravate the situation. If coverage will help rather than hurt your position, plan to present the case in a way that can be easily understood by a mass audience.

To reach a mass audience, you must first define it. Is your point of view generally popular or unpopular? Who hates it the most? Has the organization's position often been misunderstood by the public in the past, or has it been misrepresented by those who disagree with your views? In every case, write off that part of the public that cannot be reached or swayed. It is highly unlikely that the student population is going to be interested in the opening of an expensive new restaurant they can't afford. Likewise, Reagan-type Republicans aren't likely to switch their votes to a Kennedy Democrat. And don't spend an inordinate amount of time trying to convince people who agree with you anyway, although, especially in a political situation, they can't be ignored.

Usually, the people to aim for are those on the fringe, those who are leaning toward you, but are not quite there. That expensive new restaurant, for example, may well find a solid clientele among young professionals, and that Kennedy Democrat will have to go after the more conservative Democratic vote, and maybe the liberal Republican vote. Play it by ear.

On the basis of your research and organizational experience, develop a strategy and a set of tactics that will move public opinion from where it is to where you want it to be. Emotional appeal backed up with solid documentation is almost always a winning combination.

A large well-motivated crowd carrying signs and signing songs will usually attract attention. However, the repetitive use of crowd scenes to get media attention presents some hazards. For one reason it's often hard for the press to interpret accurately the meaning of a mob. There is also a tendency for one marching, singing, sign-waving crowd to look very much like the next. Finally, the media quickly catches on to what they consider to be grandstanding, and while they may cover the first demonstration, and even the second, crowd actions staged too close together look and sound too much alike, and the media will turn their attention elsewhere. An action may be most successful with mass participation, but a press conference may represent your position just as accurately and will certainly require far fewer people.

And another tip: If you intend to pack a meeting, always scout out the size of the room. If there are only 60 seats, 100 people will pack it to overflow, but 200 will leave 100 people outside and feeling excluded. Always check the size of the room in advance.

Sometimes the most effective and persuasive publicity effort is the result of one or two people or a small group operating in a situation where questions can be answered in detail, without distraction. Reporters often prefer a story that focuses on the meaning of what is being said rather than on the actions and antics of a crowd.

If an event with a large number of participants is planned, don't overlook details like parade permits and the like. The same police department that can be so unpleasant when a large crowd is sprung on them without notice may actually help clear the route if their help is requested during the planning stages of your event.

Length of Statement:

A question and answer period can last as long as reporters have questions and the speaker feels like giving answers, but a prepared statement should be *short.* Since a TV news story rarely exceeds 1½ minutes, your best chance of getting the message across uncut, with the correct emphasis, is to *keep it brief.* Press conferences should not exceed 40 minutes, from start to finish.

Celebrities:

If you want Frank Sinatra to sing Rock-a-Bye Baby at the Day Care rally, ask him. The chances are pretty good that a celebrity will say yes if he or she is in town, in sympathy with your goals, and if the date doesn't conflict with some previously scheduled engagement.

Celebrities add glamour and name appeal to almost everything, but one drawback is that they can easily steal the show. Politicians are big offenders in this area. Remind guests of the focus, and when in doubt avoid celebrities.

Celebrities are usually scheduled by their staff, management, or public relations agency. Talk with the person who actually schedules the celebrity's time, not his third cousin that Aunt Jane once met in Peoria ten years ago. You can find what celebrities will be in town on the date of your event by checking various places. Clubs and colleges frequently have prominent entertainers or speakers. Conventions also bring out big names. Also, most big city papers print a monthly schedule of coming events. The Chamber of Commerce usually keeps such a list even farther in advance.

Another way to find celebrities is by checking the coming attractions in the paper and then calling the appropriate editor to see who is handling the appearance. Be alert and don't miss opportunities for logical tie-ins. For example, a certain assembly candidate enjoyed the support of various groups of handicapped citizens. When the movie *Coming Home,* about a handicapped Vietnam veteran, opened in a nearby theater that had no access for wheelchairs, a demonstration developed. The candidate picked up a sign, and joined in. It was a good cause, and the fact that the film's two stars, Jane Fonda and Jon Voight, had also asked that the movie be moved to an accessible theater, made for good publicity all around. Ms. Fonda became a major supporter of the candidate.

Celebrities can also issue statements, endorsements, and telegrams of support. Call and ask for them in advance. If you know the people well, write the statement and ask your noted supporter to approve the text. Make each statement different.

Research:

In the planning stage, talk about not only what will be said, but how it will be substantiated. This means getting facts and figures together well in advance. Make sure that sources are generally acknowledged to be "reliable". The Bureau of Labor Statistics, the census, the *New York Times* and the *Wall Street Journal* are generally felt to be reliable sources. On the other hand, even though they may be accurate, the *Peking Review* or the newsletter of the John Birch Society do not count as reliable sources because both are widely believed to be biased.

Summarize the research in a fact sheet, and identify the source of the information.

Clipping Service:

To follow progress in the press and to help with research it is often helpful and a good investment to subscribe to a clipping service. A clipping service charges a nominal fee per month to clip articles from the papers you tell them to read. They will clip exactly what is requested, so be *explicit.*

If you only want articles in which your group, organization, politician, or whatever, and its activities are mentioned—say so. For example, if the subject is Indians, don't just ask for clips on "Indians," because you will get pictures of Tonto and the news from New Delhi. Instead specify "news and features related to American Indian health care in the Southwestern U.S."

A wire service story about your group may run in many papers. Only one clipping is necessary to verify that the story went out over the wire, however. To avoid duplication, tell the service "clip original story only."

THURSDAY: WRITTEN MATERIAL

There are only two ways to do media contact. Either the media come to you or you go to them. If they call you, have something in writing that gives a brief idea of what the organization, issue, or business is all about. If you initiate the contact, have prepared written material. This material is called the background or the handout or the release or the clips. The strategy plan should include how much and what kind of written material is needed. Delegate a person to write it and another person to clear it.

Clearing copy means that at least one other person besides the writer sees, reads, hears, and checks the accuracy of everything before it goes out. This is very important. If there is a a committee for this function, keep it small or be prepared to spend half your life arguing about the best wording for a press release—a counterproductive activity. If the person coordinating media is not in close day-to-day contact with the group, the person who clears the copy should be.

Do not flood the media with 20 pages of different colored, mimeographed propaganda filled with unsupported allegations. As far as most news desks are concerned, the Second Coming itself wouldn't need more than a one-page release. Try to keep everything to a single page.

Written material for a press conference could include a one-page release accompanied by a one-page fact sheet and perhaps one page of additional background information. (See Chapter 2.)

FRIDAY: MAIL

Now that the event is planned, and the written material is cleared, you have to mail out the notification. This is where the press list comes in. A basic news press list for a middle-sized American city usually includes 15 to 20 papers and stations. After free-lancers, underground papers, community press, stringers, and correspondents are added, the size of the list may well double.

A basic press list begins with the phone book or a standard trade listing at the library. There is nothing complicated or mysterious about this list. It contains the names of all the print and broadcast outlets in the area with a wide general audience, plus specialized trade, technical, community, or educational publications where appropriate.

Many organizations put their press list on labels. This may be helpful, but you may find, on the other hand, that you have a lot left over or that you are sending material to the wrong people. Almost every press list is a custom job that is tailored to a particular event and a specific audience. The exceptions are businesses and political candidates which rely on the same editors and reporters.

When mailing a release for a scheduled news event address the notification to the function title, not the person. Even though the city editor is a personal friend, address mail to the City Editor, or City Desk, rather than to your friend's name. This avoids having the mail sit on the desk because the editor is sick or on vacation. The following is a list of some of the titles commonly found in the communications field:

Newspapers: City desk, Sunday, women's, sports, business, editorial page, op-editorial page. In addition, most larger papers have beat writers on such subjects as: labor, health, crime, politics, science, consumer affairs, conservations, and so on.

Magazines: Editors have essentially the same functions as newspapers but have a longer lead time. Magazines seldom cover press conferences.

Television and radio: News assignment editor; producer plus time of show, such as 6 P.M. news; producer plus name of the show, such as "Sixty Minutes"; executive producer special projects; public affairs director; news director; and so on. Radio news and features have the same titles as television news and features.

Wire services, bureaus: The bureau chief

Photographers: Photo assignment editor (newspapers, magazines, bureaus, wire services)

Also always mail a release to yourself. If you don't get a release in the mail, chances are no one else did either. It is also a good indication of when to start the follow-up.

Always mail from the main post office. If releases are dumped in the corner mailbox without zip codes, it might take them a week to get across town. But if everything is zip coded and mailed form the main P.O., chances are the mail will arrive promptly the next day.

MONDAY: CHECK THE LOCATION, REHEARSE, MAKE CALLS

Check the Location

Always check the location out in advance. If it's a room, check the location of the plugs and the light switches, and the entrances, exits, stairs, phones, bathrooms, and so on; find out how to work the drapes. Remove competing or inappropriate material from the wall. If the subject is utility rate reform and the posters in the room say "GAY and PROUD" and that shows up in the TV coverage, you've got an identity problem.

Make sure to learn the name of the janitor and find out if he will be in the vicinity on the day of the event. If not locate the fuse box and determine how to replace a fuse if the television lights blow anything out.

Check the source of light in the room. Never set up a speaker's table where the speakers will have their backs to the window. If additional material will be distributed, a table by the door is handy.

If the event is on private property and the subject is controversial, it's nice to have the permission of the owner in writing. If the location is public property, like the steps of City Hall, it is customary and courteous to let the chief administrative office know you're coming.

Rehearse

Most people, no matter how well motivated, are frightened of public speaking. They don't know why they are, but they are. They are afraid they will die of a heart attack or the ground will open beneath their feet or the audience will make fun of them. These things almost never happen, though each new speaker fully expects it. One of the joys of participating in public affairs is that 90 percent of what is planned comes off if it is well rehearsed.

It is best, but not essential to practice at the actual location. All that is really necessary is for all the main people involved to get together in one place and ask each other all the nasty, loaded, snide, rude, hostile, tricky questions they can think of. At the same time, they should go on to interrupt, shine lights in each other's eyes, make loud noises in the back of the room, and click a camera up close in their faces.

Silly? Wrong. It prepares everyone for the worst. It will then be a pleasant surprise when the press shows up and is attentive and well informed, and asks all the questions you want to answer.

It may seem obvious, but it isn't necessary to be a living authority on all aspects of the subject in question. If a question is asked that is not your department, refer it to the proper person. Try not to say "no comment." That sounds defensive, and why be defensive? If you out and out don't know, say, "I don't know." If you get caught in a mistake, admit it, mistakes do happen. If you are mistaken, say, "I'm sorry but I was wrong."

Practice really makes the difference. It circumvents confusion, and the speaker always has a rough idea of what to say next. Transitions and ways to steer the discussion will come naturally. Practice a pleasant, clear, conversational tone of voice. Practice making eye contact with the person asking questions and look at the TV cameras so that all the people in television land can look you in the eye too. In the studio follow the red lights on top of the camera to know which camera is live and where to look.

After practicing, work on the answers and numbers that don't come so easily. The purpose of practice is to locate weak spots and shape them up.

Make Calls

Sometime in the early afternoon, call the people on the basic list. Say, "Hello, this is (your name). I'm calling for (name of the organization). I'd like to speak to the assignment editor. Oh, he's on another line, well maybe someone else can help me. We're having a press conference (rally, meeting, etc.) on Wednesday, Nov. 20th (date) at 9:30 A.M. (time). I've sent you a press release. Will you check your file to see if it's been received?"

Stay on the phone while the person checks the file. If it has been received say, "Thank you very much." If not ask, "Will you take a memo on it please?" Then give a slow one-minute spiel on the event, date, time, and exact location, including the room number if it is indoors. That very day send another copy of the release.

By Monday afternoon you should know that all your releases have been received and correctly filed. It is especially important that the event be listed through AP and UPI. These wire services have calendars of events called "Daybooks" or "Budgets" that are sent out every day to every major newsroom in town. If you follow up with no one else, be sure to call the wire services.

If, before making the calls on Monday afternoon, you learn that there is new information, such as that Woody Allen is going to give the opening remarks, do not keep it a secret. Add this information verbally in the follow-up calls. Sometimes its wise to plan it so there will be a few items of interest to add by phone. The trick is to have enough news and enough calls that the press is correctly led to believe that the event is of wide general interest.

TUESDAY: FINISH UP, MORE CALLS

The calls should begin about 10 A.M. the day before the event, and continue into the early afternoon. They should come from everywhere.

Make it clear to the members that the day before a press conference is a good time to call the papers, radio, and television to express interest in the forthcoming event.

The calls should take the format: "I'm so and so, I'm interested in the press conference being held tomorrow for such and such reason (I'm a member of the committee, I agree with them, I'm interested in the subject, and so on)." There is seldom a good reason to call a news outlet after 3 P.M., however, especially TV news, where tempers get short as the evening news deadline approaches.

Be personally responsible for lining up three callers besides yourself. The first caller should call the list at 10 A.M. and asks, "Are you coming? Who are you sending?" The response will be a mixture of yes-no-maybe.

Turn the results of the 10 A.M. calls over to the 11 A.M. person who calls only the no's and maybes. If they're still undecided they obviously don't know enough about it. Tell them more and tell them quickly. You usually pick up a few more yesses on this round.

At 1 P.M. you get the best "voice" to give the final pitch to the diehard holdouts. This pitch can be anything that will catch an editor's interest that hasn't already been said three times. One infallible approach is to intimate that you are from out of town and do a little writing from time to time. You have gotten wind of this press conference and are dying to cover it. "Can you help me out and tell me where it is?" Nothing gets media people interested faster than the hint that they might miss something and somebody else—God forbid, someone not from here—might get it first.

Somewhere before the end of the day go to the bank and get a roll of dimes and a roll of nickels and verify that someone is assigned to work the door tomorrow.

WEDNESDAY: THE DAY OF THE SCHEDULED NEWS EVENT

Put your rolls of change in your pocket (always wear clothes with pockets) and go to the location at least an hour before the event is scheduled. Find the janitor, open the room, and check it. Then go to the nearest phone and call the list one more time. It's handy to know the direct line to the newsrooms. Time is important now and should not be wasted waiting for the switchboard to connect you. Also, many switchboards are not open early in the morning.

These calls may appear unnecessary, but they are very important. This is your last chance to let the editor know the event is coming off as planned, and the only time to catch him when he is actually assigning for the day. These calls take about a half hour, and give you an excellent idea of what media will attend, the names of the reporters, and what aspect of the story interests the editor most.

If all is on schedule the majority of the yesses will show up. However, it's amazing how many people will hold a press conference and not keep a door list. When asked "Who was there," they won't know. When asked "were there any news stories?" they won't know either.

The person on the door keeps a list of everybody who walks

in and their affiliation. Those attending are allowed to be affiliated with themselves, or the IRS, or the group throwing the show, or to a certain extent to be among the merely curious. The purpose of the door list is to find out exactly who is there and to separate the press from the spectators.

Security:

If the subject is controversial some people may seek to disrupt your event or use it to put out their own point of view. This is yet another reason for a door list. The best way not to have disruptive kinds of trouble is to keep potential troublemakers out.

Time

Next to content, time is the most important consideration. Everything in media runs on deadlines. Those deadlines are not flexible. Try to run a tight ship and get the reputation for starting and ending on time. If the conference is scheduled to start at 9:30 and be over no later than 10:00, don't keep a dozen people waiting around just because one crew or reporter is late. At that point it's their problem. The publicist's problem is keeping the event on schedule.

At The Press Conference:

The press conference itself is usually a busy, crowded affair with those being covered feeling a little self-conscious. Mostly they go off as planned and last no more than 40 minutes.

The best press conferences are the ones where everybody feels that something of importance is happening live right in front of them.

Custom gives TV news the first shot at questions. After the lights go off there is usually a break for questions from the print media. Radio reporters and feature writers usually bring up the rear.

The publicist steers the event. He or she presumably has talked with these reporters before, and knows, too, all the participants from the organization in the spotlight. Therefore the publicist is the person qualified to match them. The youngster from the shopping news may be lovely and charming, but steer the distinguished atomic scientist to the woman from *Newsweek*. And remind the membership to follow your signals.

Visuals help relieve the tedium of talking heads. Anything with a dog or a baby stands a better chance of getting covered than anything without. Lacking an infant or canine participant, other livestock from rabbits to flamingoes are helpful. So are charts, slides, gags, stunts, tap dancing bananas, and unveiling an exact replica of the golden calf denounced by Moses. Laughter helps. The subject may be deadly serious, but it is not necessary to create an atmosphere akin to the local morgue.

Visuals:

If name recognition is important to your business or group, have lots of signs with the name on them. And remember that while visuals add interest to an event, they don't show up on radio. When referring to charts or diagrams the speaker must supply the identification: "You will see that profits start here," is a mystifying statement to a radio listener. Where is here? "You will see that oil company profits start at $600 million," makes the reference clear, even though the words "oil company profits" and "$600 million" dominate the chart.

Sound:

Speakers usually wear microphones around their necks, are provided with a stand-up mike, or are seated at a table in front of a variety of mikes. However the microphones are set up, once the speaker is in place, he or she should try not to move around, as it will result in an uneven sound level and possibly make the tape unusable.

Afterwards:

After the press conference or event is over, do not follow your natural inclination to take the rest of the day off and rehash the whole scenario with your pals. Instead call in to the contact number and pick up messages. (Naturally, someone has been covering the home front during this extravaganza.) Or better yet, return to the contact phone and stay there the rest of the day. If this is impossible, phone in at least once an hour for messages, late developments, and the like. When everything has settled back to normal, (usually somewhere around lunch time), write and clear the radio phone-in statement.

The phone-in statement goes to any radio station that did not cover the event live. Write it out and time it to run not more than 45 seconds. Then call it in to all the missing stations.

You say: "This is (your name) calling for (your organization. I'm sorry you couldn't make our press conference this morning. I'd like to give you a 45-second statement about what happened. Do you want to tape it now, or would you rather I read a couple of sentences for a sound level?"

Radio stations will almost always take a phone statement. More often than not they will run what you give them uncut; this is the easiest way known to get air time with the least effort.

Monitor Coverage and Clips

It is important to monitor the coverage. Assign members the job of watching the various news broadcasts and listening to the radio. Where did the story run? How long was it? Was it fair and accurate?

Summarize the results on a report sheet so that future coverage can be analyzed—is it getting better, worse, or staying the same?

Newspaper clippings can be very useful in the future if the story is favorable. Clip all stories. Remember to note information such as the name of the paper, the date, the section, and the page it ran on. These can later be pasted up and reproduced as clip sheets to distribute to media and others who are interested.

For an accurate record keep clips together and in chronological order. Do not loan out originals.

THURSDAY: ASSESSMENT AND THANK YOU

Spend a little time with the group and determine what could have been done differently or more effectively. This session should not be used for recriminations. It must be assumed that everybody was doing the best they could. If their best wasn't good enough, don't spend time making people feel bad. Reinforce the idea that scheduled news events are fun, easy, and useful, not that they are tense, angry affairs that end up creating enemies and hurting feelings.

By and large, people who work in the media try to do a good job. They seldom get very much feedback on the work they do, however. If someone does a good job covering the story, don't forget to say thank you. If the job is really outstanding a note to the boss is in order.

On the other hand if coverage was grossly exaggerated, biased, and unfair, wait at least 24 hours, and then complain only if necessary. Wait until you cool off to complain, and try to see it their way. If you still can't see it their way, go see the managing editor or the news director and talk it over. If there still isn't a meeting of the minds, there is always the court and the FCC.

5
Attitudes, Ethics, and Other Considerations

ATTITUDES AND ETHICS

Effective public relations requires a positive attitude and good ethics. Don't lie to the press. This doesn't mean don't evade. If reporters don't ask the right questions, it is not one's patriotic duty to shine bright lights into dim and foggy corners.

Ethical public relations means that facts are accurate and well documented, and sources are reliable. It means not dragging irrelevant facts in to damage someone for the sake of damaging. It means paying bills and returning phone calls promptly.

Over a period of time, PR people develop a personal style and credibility that does not necessarily transfer to their business or organization. Sometimes you will encounter situations whose resolutions run counter to your own best judgment. At these times it's necessary to swallow hard and put organizational or business goals ahead of personal prejudice.

On the other hand, there are times when you have to draw the line, and the line usually involves ethics and honesty. J.F. terHorst, a former presidential press secretary, set a good example for all publicists when he resigned rather than put his name to Ford's pardon of Richard Nixon, after having issued earlier assurances to the press that "no deals had been made."

A positive attitude is also essential to good public relations. The media does not operate as a propaganda service for any particular point of view. There is no vast conspiracy on the part of the media to stifle a certain cause, candidate, or business. Coverage is based on criteria such as newsworthiness, interest, timeliness, humor, and human interest. It is up to the publicist to convince the proper party, without belaboring the point, that his or her event contains one or more of these factors. Publicists are not necessarily treated gently or at length by the media, but if materials are presented well and have something pertinent to say, publicity will result. Don't despair.

Publicists should like people and should expect the best to happen rather than the worst—which is not to say the worst won't happen anyway. It also helps to be curious, polite, accurate, punctual, and tenacious. And, because PR deals with people, the ability to write well and speak easily are essential.

Proper ethics and attitude for particular types of PR will be discussed in Section II.

TIPS ON KEEPING COSTS DOWN

The best things in life are free. Unfortunately, many of the items necessary to run a campaign aren't. The following information may help you overcome this minor obstacle. Learn how to scrounge and ask for favors. While it is easy to buy your way into the public eye, it is a real challenge to arrive on a shoestring budget.

Assume a budget has been prepared, and you know approximately how much can be spent in each area, and what the publicity requirements are. It is now necessary to whittle costs as much as possible, or simply manage to make ends meet.

Nonprofit organizations can cut practically any cost. Political organizations have more difficulty, but they can do it. Small businesses have the least amount of leeway in paring the budget without sacrificing quality and effectiveness.

IN SEARCH OF FREEBIES

Be fearless in the search for freebies and cut rates. Ask for the sun, the moon, and the stars. Show no hesitation. Act as though it is the most reasonable request in the world. The worst answer one can get is no. With a little bit of luck, it's possible to get half of what you asked for. And, with God on your side, you'll get the whole enchilada. This theory works with printers, corporate executives, and movie stars. Don't be afraid to ask for help or donations, and you will probably be pleasantly surprised at the number of people who are willing to supply them. But remember: If you don't ask, how is anyone going to know what you want or need?

Also remember that when people are volunteering something, they can't be expected to give up their livelihood for the cause. Plan well in advance, and have alternatives available if volunteers can't come through.

A theater group in Berkeley, California, had a wealth of professional talent at its fingertips. People, impressed by the quality of the groups performances, had volunteered their service in various fields. Among those volunteering were a professional camera crew, who filmed a public service announcement for television. We ran into several obstacles. First, the costumes ran behind schedule. Then, the camera crew could not get the kind of camera we needed for the job. Then, a member of the crew had to go out of town on his regular job. Finally, we could not get editing facilities until almost a week and a half after we had filmed. The chairman of the Board of Directors, in sheer frustration, exclaimed "I can't even blame anyone, because no one is being paid."

This is simply the price one pays when dealing with volunteers. If the hired help screws up, they can be fired. Volunteers cannot be fired, although some should definitely be banished. But, by and large, professional people who volunteer do an excellent job, and are providing services that would probably cost a small fortune otherwise. So be understanding patient, plan alternatives, and try and be helpful.

There is also something to remember when contracting out

work that the organization is paying for. You are the boss. You are paying for a service, and you have every right in the world to expect that service to be provided in a quality manner. When requesting a quote, ask the contractor for a total job quote. If possible, get it in writing. Printers, photographers, writers, all sorts of people, may assume things that you don't. For example, a printer may give a quote assuming that the organization will provide camera-ready copy. If you don't provide it, and he must prepare it, the costs will be greater. Make sure the printer knows that he must clear any additioanl costs on the job through you. If he does not, in some states you are not obligated to pay more than 10 percent above the original quote. Be reasonable, though. Don't get a reputation for being a real nit-picker, but let contractors know that you expect quality and reasonably accurate quotes, and that you won't settle for less.

VOLUNTEERS: HOW TO GET THEM. *Volunteer* is a key word. The organization presumably has a small, hardcore group of volunteers (some professional), and possibly a small paid staff as well. But more people power is needed. Quality people power is attainable from several different sources. First, check out other organizations with goals similar to yours. If things look good, join forces. For example, a pro-choice on abortion group would be crazy not to seek the support of women's organizations, while a group desirous of saving the last surviving wallaby in the United States should definitely contact conservationists and animal lover types of organizations.

This dual effort can be mutually beneficial. First, if an organization is very small, or the cause relatively unknown, a certain degree of credibility can be attained by linking up with a larger, already recognized organization. That organization may also be able to lend the smaller one facilities, such as phones and copying equipment, until the smaller can get on its feet. The larger organization, in turn, may enlist the help of the smaller organization in the future for its cause, and in the meanwhile may enlist a little extra people power.

College and high school campuses are another good source

of volunteers. Many have intern programs that allow students to earn credits for their work with community groups and businesses. Interns can be used in everything from political campaigns to commercial PR work, with excellent results. There may be an occasional dud, but interns are usually full of energy and new ideas, and are willing to work hard. Also check out local senior citizens groups. Seniors not only make dedicated volunteers, they also add insight and experience to a campaign.

The next level of volunteer is the professional. Look within the ranks for such talent first. It also is a good idea to have everyone in the organization jot down names and phone numbers of people they know who may be able to provide special sorts of volunteer help. The number of printers, graphic artists, writers, media wizards, photographers, and other assorted and sundry people who may be at your disposal is usually impressive.

ASKING FOR HELP

The San Francisco Hookers Ball is a good example of people acquiring professional talent by asking. When the ball was in the process of becoming a San Francisco tradition, the publicists were trying to get a poster designed. Someone mentioned that David Goines, the well-known graphic artist, sometimes donated his talents to a worthy cause. (The proceeds from the ball go to the nonprofit Victoria Woodhull Foundation). The idea was tabled because nobody thought Goines would be interested in a feminist cause. This was mistake number one. Never assume such a thing. ("Doonesbury" cartoonist Garry Trudeau is a stalwart supporter of the National Women's Political Caucus, and has donated his talents on more than one occasion.) Fortunately, one of the hookers took it upon herself to call on Mr. Goines, who agreed to design his "Queen of Hearts" poster for the Ball.

The same asking theory works on big name movie stars,

writers, politicians, athletes, and rock stars. Don't be afraid to ask. They can be had. But remember that these people are on strenuous schedules: they can hardly be expected to fit in a Friday appearance at the Weekly Society to Prevent Cruelty to Penguins if you call on the preceding Wednesday.

Call as far ahead as possible. Contact either the agent or the press secretary, and present the request and a date. Be ready to send background information, as it will probably be requested.

It may be necessary for the organization to provide lodgings and other necessities for the visiting dignitary. Plan the celebrity's stay so that it is as easy from their point of view as possible. Don't schedule a press conference, a briefing, and dinner with the local powers all within an hour after the plane lands. Celebrities are human. They need time to breathe, and they need as much privacy as possible. In other words, don't throw open the doors to the public at any time other than the public function. Hold the groupies and autograph hounds at bay, even if one of them happens to be your best friend. Remember, if you want star power in the future, make the situation that you bring them into livable. If you don't, the next invitation may be tossed unopened into the garbage can, no matter how worthy the cause.

PRINTED MATERIALS

Printing is another good place where you can save money. A good bit of it is necessary, and it can be one of the most expensive items in the campaign. For example, one of the first items any organization needs is letterhead and envelopes. Keep the logo simple. Nothing looks tackier than cutesy animals or esoteric symbols fussing around at the top of a press release. Don't waste a graphic artist's talents on letterhead, unless there is money to burn. Many quick print places have both a nice selection of lettering that is adequate and inexpensive paper. Use your own judgment. Make sure that the name of the organization, the address, and the phone number are on the letterhead and on the envelope. Select a paper stock and lettering that are in common use. Then, if the supplier is on vacation, or temporarily out of what you are using, it is easier to find the same items elsewhere.

A brochure is another necessary item. The absolute, rockbottom cheapest form is white stock, black ink, and no photographs. Unfortunately, this makes for a boring brochure in most cases, although not always. However, there are a few things that may create a more exciting brochure for very little extra money.

The first thing is to sit down and talk with the printer *before* getting camera-ready copy. Don't believe anything graphic artists say about cost. They are interested in creating a masterpiece, and the budget is of very little concern to them, as long as they get paid. They will undoubtedly create a fantastic piece, but it won't do much good if it gets to the printer who says that the special typeface, the mixed tint ink, the three-color requirement, the five photos, the coated paper, and the odd size are going to bring the brochure in at about $1000 over budget. If this happens, it's back to the drawing board to straighten things out; this process, too, is going to cost money, but not as much.

Get basic ideas from the graphic artist, therefore, and then discuss matters with your printer. If you can actually get the two together for a meeting, so much the better. If this isn't possible, here are a few basic things you should remember. Black ink is the cheapest, and one-color printing is the cheapest. The industry standard for ink selection is PMS. Any printer should have a sample book of these colors. True colors are cheaper than tints or shades. Two colors of ink increase expenses, because the piece must be run through the press again to apply the second color. Likewise for third and fourth colors. Each additional run through the press costs more money.

Paper cost varies primarily according to "weight" and whether or not the paper or stock is coated. Coated stock, which has a shiny finish, is much more expensive than regular matte finished stock, and it should not be chosen unless you are being backed by a billionaire. Choose the stock you want by weight. The "weight" of a particular piece of paper is based on the weight of 1000 of the parent sheets from which it is cut. Confusing, right? That's why we simplify things. Basically, all you need be concerned with is book, cover, and index weights. Most of these move up in 10-pound increments, with the higher increment being the heavier stock. Book weight is the lightest, and is suitable for flyers, letters, and that sort of printed matter. If the piece must survive the rigors of the U.S. mail, or door-to-door handout, it's best to go to an index or cover weight. Again, the printer should have samples. Give him or her an approximate cost range, and ask to see samples within that range. You should be able to find something nice that will still fit into the budget.

Size and shape influence cost, too. Naturally, the larger the piece, the greater the expense. But remember that an odd size or cut can add a lot to costs also. And there can also be problems with the mail, if the piece is for mailing. Call the post office and make sure that they will accept the size piece (folded) that you have in mind. One organization spent approximately $1500 on a beautiful self-mailer, only to find out that the post office would not accept it. So be careful. The number of times the piece is folded will also add to the cost, which increases with each fold. Try to stick to a simple one or two folds. Money can also be saved by using self-mailers as opposed to envelopes. Print your message on one side, and reserve space on the other side for an address label.

There is one other way to save a great deal of money on stock. Printers will often run an odd-sized piece for someone with more money than sense. This results in scraps. Quite often, those scraps can serve quite nicely for the purpose you have in mind. During a political campaign in Oakland, California, for example, a walking piece was needed—something that precinct organization members could carry in their hand door to door, and that could also be put into legal sized envelopes. Someone had run an odd-sized job that left scraps slightly smaller than a legal envelope, and the publicists grabbed them, thereby cutting printing costs by almost $300.

It was also a much better quality of stock than the campaign directors could have otherwise afforded. It pays to be on good terms with printers.

Finally, corporations, individuals, church groups, or some well-intentioned being may provide stock. Usually, it will be in the form of blank 8½-×-10 sheets that can be used for letter-head and envelopes. But you may luck out and get something that will be a good weight for brochures too.

Print itself can also affect costs. Typesetting is almost always more expensive than offset, but it also looks nicer. Reserve this for more important pieces. If you are reproducing a letter or flyer, definitely go with offset printing. Any copying place can usually provide this service, and in quantity, it is less expensive than copying. Again, try to stay with a fairly common type if the piece is typeset, so that you can go to another printer if necessary.

One way to achieve a dramatic looking black and white piece is by using a "reverse-out." This procedure reverses the printing process, with white lettering jumping out of a black back-ground. It is only slightly more expensive that a regular black ink, white background piece, and is doubly dramatic. However, it is hard on the eyes, and therefore not advisable for small print or lengthy brochures. You can also reverse out with any other ink color, but again, the cost increases.

Another inexpensive way to add color is to select colored stock. Stick to basic colors and the additional expense is mini-mal, and is usually more than worth it.

Photographs will also add to the cost of the printed piece, and again, the increase is per photo. Black and white is cheapest. Don't use colored stock if you are using photos with people's faces. The faces will end up being unbecoming shades of puce and violet, and will make the public not want to proceed fur-ther.

Talk with the photographers, and make sure they understand exactly what you want. In fact, go along on the shooting session if possible. Choose photos with high contrast, especially if they will be reproduced in newspapers. Keep them as uncluttered as possible.

MAILING

If you are putting out a number of mailings consisting of more than 200 pieces at each shot, by all means get a bulk rate stamp. The post office has a package available that explains very clearly how to prepare bulk mailings. This clarity is unusual for the post office, and you should take advantage of it for that reason if for no other. Just remember to mail the piece at least two weeks ahead of the date that it should arrive, since bulk rate is not first class mail.

Be forewarned that you will come across someone—an artist, printer, typesetter—who will find a problem not covered here, probably one that is unique. Just play it by ear. You should now have enough basic information to make a wise and economically feasible decision.

Run the total number of pieces required, if at all possible, on the first press run. It is much cheaper to have one run of 500 pieces that to have two runs of 250 pieces.

OFFICE SUPPLIES

Whether the office is in someone's kitchen, or in a storefront, you are going to need paper clips, rubber bands, pencils, typing paper, typewriters, desks, and all the other supplies of a regular office.

Ask local corporations for them, beginning with the employers of the members of your group. Ask if they can contribute a couple of boxes of rubber bands or pencils, or a ream of typing paper. These are minor expenses for most businesses, but can put a nonprofit organization in the poorhouse. Unless the cause is particularly unpopular, it is possible to come up with a goodly supply of earthly goods. If the cause is unpopular, just be more creative in your methods of obtaining them. Don't rob office supply stores, but do start saving the rubber bands from your daily newspaper and from vegetables. Pick up paper clips from the gutter. Hit wealthier members for donations. An office doesn't run without supplies, so accept the fact, and get busy.

BILLBOARDS

This section applies to nonprofit organizations only, since political and business entities just have to fork out the bucks for billboard space and printing costs. Nonprofit groups can contact the local billboard people, and ask what their requirements are for obtaining free space. They will probably want some background information on the group, the nonprofit number, and some indication as to how many billboards you would like in what locations. Remember that the billboard companies get thousands of requests each year for free space, so make the group sound as broad-based and exciting as possible. Usually, the company will provide the space for free, and sometimes include the assistance of one of their graphic artists as well. Your organization will probably have to pay labor costs, however, unless something is worked out with the local union in charge of putting up billboards.

Once space and labor are acquired, you will have to deal once again with a printer. Ask the billboard company to recommend printers, since billboards require special presses.

Billboards are like brochures in that black and white, without photos is the cheapest. Again, the best bet is to sit down with all involved, and work out the specifics. Choose locations carefully to coincide with an audience who will be responsive. If you are a theater group, and there is a theater district in your city, try to get at least one board placed there. If you are an antidraft group in a college town, try to get a placement in the vicinity of the campus. Main thoroughfares and freeway on-ramps and off-ramps are good for just about any cause.

Remember that the basic billboard costs are: space, art work, printing, and labor. Be sure to cover the bases in each area.

This same sort of strategy applies to bus signs and other public advertising spaces. Check out the specifics with the local transportation or municipal authorities. Quite often, there are city or state regulations governing the posting of printed materials in public places. Be sure that these requirements are met. It would be depressing to have materials ready, only to discover that one minor detail prevents them from being placed before the public.

UNION SHOP VS. LABOR DONATED

It is easy to get into trouble with a union, especially if you are a political group or candidate. One sure way to lose the union vote is to put out a major piece of literature without a "union bug." A union bug is a small emblem, placed in an inconspicuous place, that indicates that the piece was printed by a union shop.

Most nonprofit groups can avoid this quandry by printing "Labor Donated" at the bottom of the piece, and the same procedure can be followed by politicians for minor pieces such as flyers, handouts, and fund-raising letters. But little can help the candidate, especially the Democratic candidate, if a fancy flyer goes out without a union bug. The same holds true for any business that deals with unions. So stay alert, and be sure that, if you don't have a bug, you have "Labor Donated."

WHAT TO DO IN A CRISIS:

THE "DOOMSDAY CHECKLIST"
Borrowed from The Foundation for American Communications in North Hollywood, California, the checklist contains 12 points for dealing with the immediacy of any crisis:
  1. Set up an emergency service notification system. (a) Who notifies the PR person. (b) Whom does PR notify. Include phone numbers.
  2. Set up a list of who to notify in the organization, complete with phone numbers.
  3. Name a designated spokesperson and phone number.
  4. Choose a location in advance for press conference or media set-up.
  5. Set up a media notification list, plus phone numbers.

6. Have backround information on hand for reporters.
7. Provide information to date on the crisis, which you and your organization have reviewed together.
8. Arrange for additional news availability via a news conference, spokesperson, or other.
9. Provide follow-up information and answers to questions that could not be answered during the first stage of the crisis, such as how it will impact the organization or business and what are final determinations as to financial loss, injuries, deaths.
10. Monitor and report to media on further and unfolding developments as they occur following organizational review.
11. Outline and review total procedural approach including all phases of news gathering and distribution. (Be alert as to protection of sensitive or damaging information.)
12. Do a postcrisis analysis of every step, including your own performance. This is a must for improving the handling of future crises.

BASIC GUIDELINES FOR WRITING NEWS ABOUT WOMEN
Issued by Stanford University Women's News Service 1974

Since the way women are written about is in transition one way to be sure you do not inavertently offend is to follow these or similar guidelines when you prepare copy about women. If you find that stories about women are written in a manner that you find unacceptable it is a good idea to go in and talk to the editor and suggest suitable guidelines.

1. A woman's marital status should not be indicated by a prefix attached to her name. First reference should include a person's title, if any, and given name. Later references should include last name only. For example; Rep. Bella Abzug, D-NY, said today . . . Abzug stated. Secretary of State Vance announced . . . Vance replied. Use of "Mr." and "Mrs." is limited to

discussions which include a married couple, where the last name only rule might cause confusion. Miss and Ms. should not be used at all.

2. Females over the age of 18 are "women." They are not "girls" "gals," or "ladies." Words like "homemaker" and "housewife" are not synonyms for "woman"; check carefully for accuracy before they are used. "Coed" does not mean "woman" any more than "ed" means "man"; persons who attend school are "students."

3. Gratuitous physical description, uncommon almost to the point of absence in news stories about men, should also be eliminated from stories about women. This rule does not apply with equal force to feature writing, especially profiles in which physical description is often an essential aspect. However, care should be taken to avoid stereotypical descriptions in favor of describing an individual's unique characteristics.

4. Similar considerations apply to the mention of an individual's spouse and family. In a news story, a man's wife and family are typically mentioned only in passing and only when relevant; the same practice should apply to news stories about women. And again, the practice is slightly different for feature stories and profiles but the test of relevance should always be applied.

5. Most achievents do not need sexual identification; those which do should be so identified for both men and women. Do not say: Arthur Ashe is one of the best American tennis players and Billie Jean King is one of the best women tennis players. Say either: Arthur Ashe and Billie Jean King are two of the best American tennis players, or Arthur Ashe is one of the best men tennis players and Billie Jean King is one of the best women tennis players. Do not say: Gail Thain Parker is a dynamic woman college president; Say: Gail Thain Parker is a dynamic college president.

6. Avoid sins of omission as well as those of commission. If, for example, an expert is sought in a given field, or if an example is needed to make a point, women should be used in these cases as a matter of course—not simply as "oddities" or representatives of "a woman's viewpoint."

7. Women's professional qualifications or working experience should always be acknowledged.

8. The term *women's libber* should not be used. It has no informational content and is simply a blanket perjorative.

9. When you have completed a story about a woman, go through it and ask yourself if you have written about a man in the same style.

SECTION II: SPECIFIC EXAMPLES

6

PR for Small Businesses: Beyond the Yellow Pages

Unless a small business is located in a town where every commercial venture is situated within three blocks of the other on main street, public relations will play a big part in letting the public know that it exists.

The owner should think of PR as an ongoing process that will keep the business in the public eye, create goodwill within the community and among the company's employees, and establish credibility and a clear image of the product or service rendered.

PR can also be a way to solve problems as well as a way to relate to the public. In fact, adversity is sometimes the basis of a good PR campaign.

This chapter will provide the entrepreneur with PR basics for identifying the correct market, creating goodwill via give-aways and donations, throwing a gala grand opening, and remaining in the public eye through such standard methods as news releases about new personnel and new products. It also doesn't hurt for future Henry Fords to make public appearances—giving a speech, for example, at the local Lions Club.

Publicity results from a public relations program involving reports of business activities that are deemed newsworthy by the media. An article and/or photograph about the opening of a new store, sponsorship of a charitable event, or participation by the business staff in some community action will tell people more about you.

Publicity means attracting proper attention and gaining positive exposure for the business. The more the public knows, the more they'll buy.

IDENTIFYING THE MARKET

A person directly involved in a business can often be its best PR person. Suppose you are at a party and someone asks, "What do you do?" The answer can be "I'm a caterer." Or the answer can be "I have a sensational catering business. Our specialty is Armenian hors d'oeuvres—thanks to my grandmother who has all these incredible recipes. We even take her along to some of the parties. . . . she loves being involved and guests love the stories she tells about some of the food items!"

Granted, that may be a bit effusive, but it makes the point in a positive, interesting way. Besides being generally enthusiastic and positive about your business to the outside world, you should also do a very thorough evaluation of the market. Get out a piece of paper and make a list of all the good things about the business. What makes it better than the competition? Is it open longer hours? Have the owner and staff had more experience? Is the product of a better quality? Cheaper?

Now make a list of goals that will improve sales or public image. Examples are: more black people as customers; greater employee enthusiasm; getting mentioned by a prominent columnist.

Third, list who the customers actually are. Do they tend to be old or young, male or female, of a particular ethnic or religious persuasion? How about gays? Education and economic class? What about their interests? Are they interested in sports? Do they like animals? Do they have a sense of humor? Then, on the same piece of paper write the kinds of people you'd like to have as customers but don't at present.

Congratulations! A classy PR agency would have charged $60 an hour to identify or "target" the business's market. All subsequent PR should be aimed at reaching the targeted market.

IMAGE AS PR

Before calling in the cameras to take pictures for the evening news, take a good look at the physical work environment. Is it clean and neat? How does it look? Is the nature of the business obvious, or could it be doing anything from selling clothing to fencing hot merchandise? Public relations goes beyond sending out press releases. It is up to the owner to make sure that the business is presentable once the press arrives.

A business sign should define the goods or services offered. Sometimes a window display makes it obvious, and sometimes it must be spelled out. "Galleria Zamora" could by anything from art work to exotic dancers. But "Galleria Zamora: Authentic Romanian Folk Art & Clothing" tells the story.

Likewise, the logo (which identifies the business on paper— either by a symbol or by a certain type style) should be consistent with what is offered. It should have a clean, sharp, professional look. It can be repeated not only on letterhead and envelopes, but on bags, boxes, and other containers that will be visible when carried down the street.

CREATING NEWS

It behooves the up-and-coming entrepreneur to keep a close eye on the news. Opportunities often arise that allow the small business owner to take advantage of a current situation in order to better the business. Sometimes a small expenditure is required, and sometimes it won't cost a cent. The following examples will show how a news story, election day, and adversity can all be used to gain positive PR.

GRANNY GOOSE TO THE RESCUE

Granny Goose is a company that makes potato chips and other snack food items, sold primarily in the state of California. The company has a goose suit, which a human can wear, that looks just like their logo: a fluffy goose with spectacles, a bonnet, bright orange legs and galumphing shoes.

One day the evening news carried a sad story. In the dead of night, someone had slipped off a boat in Marin County, California and onto the beach and had killed one of the geese that had been living there. The poor critter had actually been barbequed and eaten! And perhaps saddest of all, this atrocious act had the heart-rendering consequence of depriving the slain goose's mate of her eyes—she was blind.

The Marin Humane Society (MHS) took the blind goose to its shelter and announced plans to investigate the unfortunate incident and bring the perpetrator of the crime to justice. MHS is a nonprofit organization that relies totally on community support. Luckily they had in their employ a seasoned publicist, who instantly alerted the media of the goose's plight. He also seized the opportunity, as spokesperson for the organization, to give extensive media interviews, via phone calls he initiated, asking that goose lovers—and indeed all those eager for justice —make contributions so that "Goosey" could find a new home and the Humane Society could launch a thorough investigation.

What an opportunity for Granny Goose! It was decided that Granny would make a cash contribution in memory of the lost goose and in recognition of the good works of the MHS. In return, the company publicists asked that Granny (the person in the goose suit) be allowed to attend the press conference when the MHS announced Goosey's fate.

The news story about the goose murder appeared on a Friday. By Monday the MHS had decided to return Goosey to her native beach habitat the following day. All the media were notified. On Monday night, the MHS publicist gave about a dozen radio interviews announcing the plans and hinting that the name of the culprit would be announced by the District Attorney on the same day. What excitement!

On Tuesday morning, Goosey's little cove in Tiburon was teeming with newspeople—TV cameras, wire service photographers, reporters from all over the Bay Area. As the white-jacketed vets from the MHS brought Goosey down to the beach and the cameras clicked and hummed, Granny Goose was waddling right alongside. As the blind goose was released into the water she was immediately joined by a flock of ducks to guide her reentry, and Granny Goose stood on the beach waving goodbye. It made memorable TV news. Cameras still humming, Granny then presented her donation to the Humane Society. Photos of the event were taken and sent to every paper that did not send a photographer, to all animal-related publications, and to business and food trade publications, Granny Goose made the news and created a public image of being a good samaritan as well.

"THERE'S A SMALL HOTEL . . . ON ELECTION DAY"

When an advertising genius also owns a strangely unique hotel, all kinds of things are bound to happen. The Mansion Hotel, a Victorian jewel of a place resurrected from a decaying rooming house, illustrates how a small business owner can use a special day to make big news.

When the registrar of voters called upon the Mansion Hotel to open its doors to the voters of the precinct as a polling place, owner Bob Pritikin decided to create a huge news event. He sent out a press release calling the Mansion "America's Most Posh Polling Place." Pritikin proceeded to install one hundred American flags in the courtyard, dress his son up like Uncle Sam, serve red, white, and blue doughnuts on silver trays, and conjur the ghost of John Phillip Sousa to play patriotic marches on the piano. Voters would decide their fate under crystal chandeliers—a far cry from the traditional dank and smelly basements where they usually cast ballots.

On special days and assorted holidays such as election, Easter, Christmas, and Halloween, the press loves to cover interesting, poignant, or unusual events. Election day was perfect for the Mansion, as it gave television stations something to air while reporting the returns.

America's most posh polling place made it into Walter Cronkite's newscast, the front page of the *San Francisco Examiner,* and, thanks to the UPI wire photos, into hundreds of small papers across the land. The trick was calling in UPI the day before the election to photograph Uncle Sam, arms raised, on the steps of the hotel under a banner that proclaimed, "Cast Your Fate, Vote Here Nov. 7." Thus, editors got the photo on election night eve, allowing them to run the story on election day, when it was relevant and timely.

If a story with a good photo is related to a special day, have it taken the day before. On the press release, indicate that what you are doing is a "good photo opportunity" and that special arrangements can be made to shoot in advance by phoning the contact. If a costume is involved, it's a good idea to pin the media to a specific time. You might lose the coverage if they show up and you're not ready; conversely, nobody wants to sit around all day in a hot, itchy bunny suit waiting for the media.

On the other hand, patience may be required to obtain television coverage. On this election day, for instance, TV assignment editors were sending out crews to film people in various voting situations, and didn't know exactly when their reporters could come by the Mansion. It all depended on what else was going on and when they might be in the neighborhood.

One station did confirm early, requesting the opportunity to do their noon news on election day live from "America's most posh polling place." This is called a "live remote." Check with the news producers at local TV stations to see if any of them do this. If you have some unusual decor or an event going on, it might make an interesting opportunity for a live-on-location telecast. Send a note to the appropriate producer explaining why your establishment would make a dandy site for one of these.

"THERE'S A SMALL HOTEL" . . . . . IN TROUBLE!

Hard times may not be so hard if you can use them to get your name in the paper. Again, the Mansion Hotel makes a nice case history.

When the city bureaucrats threatened to shut down his little gem of a hotel—its murals depicting the history of San Francisco, its free magic concerts, its celebrity guests, and its glorious sculpture gardens notwithstanding, Bob Pritikin took his case to the media.

Located in a residential area, the Mansion Hotel was bothersome to a couple of neighbors (a "tiny band of nattering, nit-picking nincompoops," according to Pritikin) who discovered that the hotel was in violation of a recently revised planning code. They alerted the authorities—the same authorities who had originally issued him a permit and bona fide hotel license. And a red tape battle began. The fight to save the Mansion was on.

Nothing pleases the news media as much as reporting a controversy. It also makes fine editorial fodder against bungling bureaucrats in city agencies, who turn well-meaning entrepreneurs into victims of the system.

The first step was to contact a good feature writer whom it was thought might be sympathetic. What resulted was a long piece entitled "Red Tape Battle over Unique Hotel" in the *San Francisco Chronicle.* The day before the story hit the streets, we sent out press releases informing the media that Pritikin would hold a press conference at the Mansion. When the story broke in the morning paper, the rest of the media responded by attending the press conference in droves.

The release itself was full of quotable quotes. In addition to color, Pritkin had also contacted a number of high-ranking city officials, including the mayor and the District Attorney, who were mentioned as staunch supporters, thus giving the whole affair an air of credibility.

There was full-blown coverage of the Mansion controversy, and every time Pritikin went before the Planning Commission for a hearing, the press was there. They were there because it was a continuing story. They were there because Pritikin had made a mammoth mounted display of letters of support and had rounded up his friends to appear at the hearings carrying signs with variations of "Save the Mansion" written on them.

He also brought a number of his employees dressed in Victorian costume as something for the cameras to photograph, which they did, time after time.

Pritikin's three-year nightmare ended when the Mansion was declared an historical landmark, a decision that allowed it to operate as a hotel despite the planning code violation. On the day the Mayor signed the paper declaring the Mansion and ten other structures historical landmarks, the Mansion was again the subject of major news coverage. The press was invited to witness the dedication to "landmark luncheon" at the Mansion with the Mayor and a number of other celebrity supporters. And while there were ten other buildings of equal stature, the story once again focused on the Mansion.

In other words, an unjust law suit, a foreclosure, or a disaster at your place of business may provide PR potential. Think of an event or something to tell the media that will arouse the interest of both the reporter and the general public. For instance: A broken water pipe causes a big flood. Have a flood sale immediately. Rent life rafts and candles and have it at night. Invite the press. When the local Mom-and-Pop store is being robbed and an employee thwarts the culprit by bopping him on the head with a loaf of french bread—call the city editor and give all the details, including the fact that you will give a free loaf of bread to anyone presenting a clipping of the story. Heroism and danger make news. Don't overlook any opportunity to make make the "little guy" a winner over adversity.

PERSONNEL RELEASES, NEW PRODUCT RELEASES, AND HUMAN INTEREST OR APPLICATION ARTICLES

Personnel releases, new product releases, and human interest or application articles are the basics for the small business. Employees represent a business as much as its products or services, and special ones should be introduced to the public via the personnel release. If the business is just opening, send the release to the editor and/or business editor of the local paper about four weeks before the scheduled opening date. Include the person's name and position, and background information, such as past experience, college attended, marital status, number of children, current or past community involvement, and organizational memberships. Also include any unusual hobbies or accomplishments, such as Jane Doe is the current judo champion for the state of Iowa. A head and shoulders photo should also be included. Don't forget to identify it with a type-written sheet attached to the back.

The same type of release should be sent out whenever there is a new addition to management, or a promotion. (Notice of a promotion should include the former position as well as the new one.) These releases can also be sent to trade magazines. The headline for these releases should be in the form of a simple announcement: "FRANK SMITH JOINS MANAGEMENT AT UNION STREET TENNIS SHOP."

New product releases can be used by any business that constantly upgrades or develops new products. Small computer businesses are a prime example. If the previous personal computer accommodated four users, but this capacity has now been upgraded to eight, by all means notify the press. The release must describe the nature of the upgrade, tell a little about the computer and who can use it, and explain why it is now bigger, better, cheaper, or whatever. Again, the headline should take a simple announcement form. Send a photo. Distribute to the local and trade press.

Application articles can often be placed in trade journals. These are exactly what they say. For example, Susie's Body Builders announced its new machine to improve the bust six months ago, and there are now a number of happy 34 D's who will guarantee that the product works. Contact Susie's, and find a customer who is willing to tell how she used the machine, what the results are, and how it has changed her life. These stories usually run five to eight pages and take the following format: introduction, definition of the problem, other methods that didn't work, and how Susie's bust builder was used and did work. Mention the product in the first or second paragraph, but avoid using it every other line, and avoid spectacular adjectives. Otherwise, the editor will ask that an ad be taken out.

Human interest stories are another good way to get coverage. Is there someone or something in your business that makes a good story? If so, don't keep it a secret. Take, for example, a little boutique called Zamoras, which specialized in folkloric costumes and hand-embroidered clothing from Rumania. What they were selling wasn't news. How they got what they were selling, however, was. A press release was put together that told the "amazing story of Zamora" and how she traveled through the backreaches of Transylvania, trading her knapsack, her boots, and sometimes literally the shirt off her back to peasants for some of their unique hand-crafted items. During her travels, Zamora also heard many versions of the vampire legend. This landed her on a number of talk shows and got the fashion editor of the local paper interested enough to do a big feature story.

Then there was a successful class action attorney who decided to open a gourmet wine and cheese store. He had been making homemade wine in his basement for years. He was also lucky enough to win a liquor license in the state lottery. The headline of the press release read: "A LA CARTE, NORTHERN CALIFORNIA'S LARGEST INTERNATIONAL GOURMET STORE: A DREAM COME TRUE FOR LOCAL ATTORNEY" The press liked the personal angle.

People make news. Like the old Swedish woodworker who came out of retirement to create the interior of a new restaurant; the Mexican mother of the restaurant's owner who came in one Saturday to show the chef (and a number of reporters) how to make huevos rancheras the authentic way; the director of a running clinic's heroic battle to become the first woman to finish the country's most challenging marathon race; the president of a natural cosmetic company who introduced his product by showing people his little jars in bus depots, in airplanes, and in restaurants.

Whatever the business, you can get more mileage out of PR by giving the press good stories about the people involved.

GIVEAWAYS, DONATIONS, AND SPONSORSHIPS

GIVEAWAYS

Giving something away, either product or advice, can not only create goodwill and visibility, but can also actually bring people into the business establishment.

Giving away Products

Hastings Clothing Store ran an advertising campaign featuring billboards and ads showing a model sandwiched within a hot dog roll. The message: "GET YOUR BUNS TO HASTINGS AUGUST SALE." To supplement the campaign, Hastings had a "Hot Dog Day at Hastings." Free hot dogs and buns were obtained from a local company in exchange for the promise to use their name in all the publicity. The publicists rented a portable Coleman stove, and bought some napkins, mustard, ketchup, and relish. They then printed a flyer saying, "Get your buns to Hastings at noon on August 23 and get a free hot dog." Suzi Skates was hired to roll around the downtown area the morning of the event and distribute a thousand flyers.

By noon, the line in front of Hastings went around the block; 1000 hot dogs were served in just one hour. A lot of folks kept munching right on into the store. The entire event cost $66, and the resulting sales more than paid for it.

A note on food giveaways in non-retail establishments: Check with the local department of health. You may need a special permit, especially if you cooking something on public property (the sidewalk in front, for example).

However, it's tough to give away food or for that matter, just about anything, on the streets. There's an old story about a bet made between two PR people: One bet the other $100 that he couldn't give away ten $10 bills in an hour. Guess who won? This may not have actually happened, but it is a fact that 1000 Chinese fortune cookies are stored because they couldn't be given away. To promote the opening of an Exhibit of Arts and Crafts from the People's Republic of China, the publicists had thousands of fortune cookies made. The slips of paper inside read: "Good fortune will come to all who visit the Exhibition of the People's Republic of China, Sept. 13–28". No one wanted to take a cookie from a stranger.

So when thinking food or other handouts, do it inside the store. Or better yet, give things away with a purchase. That way, you are making money and people will still feel they are getting something for nothing.

Giving away advice

Making your customers feel good about you is as important an aspect of public relations as getting your name in the paper. If you can't afford to give away merchandise, hot dogs, or money, how about advice? Flower shops can give away information sheets on plant care. Dog clipping services can give away a guide to proper grooming at home. Recycled paper companies can give away instruction on how to make origami (the Japanese art of paper folding) swans

Perhaps a friend, relative, or employee is an expert in something related to your business. Having them show their expertise on your premises could benefit everyone. For example, a men's clothing store was convinced to hire a woman fashion consultant over the Christmas season. She would help women who were shopping for men. She was also in the process of launching her own consulting business, so any resulting publicity would be good for both.

Every year a hardware store in San Francisco produces a "home improvement weekend," where employees and outside professionals set up booths in the parking lot and actually show people how to lay tile, paint moldings, clean storm windows, repair garden hoses, fix leaky sinks, install deadbolt locks, and so on. Posters are displayed in the store weeks ahead, and the event is listed in the calendar section of the local papers. Consumer reporters mentioned the event on the air before it happened and subsequently covered it as a news story.

The how-to market is still booming, as evidenced by the plethora of advice columns and the number of talk show guests who impart helpful information as opposed to funny chitchat. If the general public would be interested in or would benefit from your expertise in your field, then by all means try and establish yourself as a regular "guest expert" on a local talk show. Get someone to contact the producer and make a pitch for you. Have them go in armed with a neatly produced resumé or background sheet (one page), any newspaper clippings of stories in which you have been quoted, a flattering photo, and a list of things you can talk about. If you are actually called in for an interview, make sure you rehearse a tight, vibrant three-minute presentation of what you might say on the air.

Another possibility is a weekly (monthly) column in the local newspaper or magazine. That's harder—especially if you don't have a gaggle of journalistic credentials. But it's certainly worth a shot. Look at the other columns the paper prints—pet care advice, gardening tips, whatever—and write a sample column or two of similar length. Get some help if necessary. If you think there's even the slightest possibility the editor will be impressed, go for it.

DONATIONS AND SPONSORSHIPS.

Sooner or later, a business will be asked to donate something to someone's worthy cause: the church raffle, the PBS-TV station's auction, or whatever. Or you may be hit up to sponsor an event intended to raise money for groups like the Boy Scouts or the March of Dimes.

Before you part with money or merchandise, find out what's in it for the business, beyond a tax-deduction. If you truly support the cause, then love is all you need. However, you can reap some publicity benefits if you know waht to ask for.

For instance, what sort of promotion is the organization intending to do? Press releases? Flyers? Posters? Mailings? Radio spots or newspaper ads? Will your name be mentioned?

How prominently? Will your merchandise or service be clearly identified as yours? Will you get a receipt? A thank-you letter you can frame and display in your place of business? Will there by any press people invited to the event you are sponsoring (meaning that you are underwriting the costs) or to which you are donating? Is the organization going to have someone there to take photos? Will they send one to you and to appropriate media who weren't there?

If they aren't taking pictures, consider getting a photographer yourself. The local paper might not send a reporter to cover the Police Activities League raffle, but they might run a photo if it were accompanied by the following story/caption.

"CHIEF GAINES'S TIRED TOOTSIES GET A WORK-OUT: Evan Smith (right) of Compton's Reflexology Center is pictured here with Police Chief Charles Gaines, who won an hour's worth of foot massage as one of the prizes donated by local businesses at the Police Activities League raffle held last week at the Elks Hall" Photo credit: Julie Smith.

There. You've gotten your name in the paper, along with the PAL and the Chief. Nicely done.

When sponsoring an event, try to get your money back in terms of publicity. That's a hard thing to calculate, but let's say the March of Dimes wants you to kick in $500 to sponsor a racquetball tournament (you are essentially covering their up-front costs for T-shirts, facility rental, poster production, mailing of announcements and press releases, etc.). If you're relatively new in town and want name recognition, then reaching 1000 people will cost you 50¢ a person and may be well worth it. However, you might not not want to spend more than a nickel just to have someone see your name on a flyer. In that case, figure out if the publicity efforts of the March of Dimes will allow 10,000 people to know that you are their event's sponsor in order to make the donation mean something. In any case, insist that your name be connected with the event in the first sentence of any material sent to the media. A mention at the bottom of a press release or calendar announcement allows an editor's blue pencil to make it disappear from the copy.

Be present at the event itself or send a representative, preferably with some literature or information about the business or service or with samples of the products.

WORTH 1,000 WORDS: PHOTO STORIES

If you can't think of a stupendous event that will bring the press out to take pictures, take them yourself and send them in. Newspapers use "cute," "interesting," and "timely" (connected with a holiday or related to current news events) photos more often than you realize. It may be something simple like a cat napping on a typewriter; something poignant like an elderly couple holding hands in front of your store; something holiday-related like kids trick-or-treating in your business; or something funny like a sign on your door that says "Out feeding the rhino. Back in 10 minutes (I hope)."

All of these situations have the potential of turning up as a photo story in the paper. Use a good 35 mm camera and have an 8-×-10 glossy print done by a professional photofinisher. Attach a caption to it (one paragraph) that tells the story, gives the date, and mentions your business. Although it may not be used, give whomever took the picture a photo credit, and don't forget to identify everyone from left to right. Also, if you are taking a candid shot of people you don't know, ask for their permission to use the photo.

Sometimes the wire services (AP or UPI)—if your town has any—take photos and distribute them to newspapers all over the world through their electronic photowire machine. They may rewrite your caption to conform with their own particular style. But if that photo winds up in 100 papers across the land, let them at it.

Newspapers have a photo morgue with lots of things they can pull out to use when they aren't filled up with editorial copy. Contact the photo editor of your local newspaper. Let him or her know you've got a good photo you'd like to send them and that you hope they'll use it sometime.

Check your newspaper for the kinds of things they run and the length of their photo captions. That will give you a good idea of what they are apt to use. Here's an example: You own a repair service. You also have a pet parrot. One day the parrot gets out of the cage and is sitting on a car fender looking under the raised hood. Grab your camera. Here's the caption:

Polly Wanna Crankcase?
Modesto, July 5, 1980—At Zeke's garage, business was for the birds today as Polly, the pet parrot decided to lend a helping beak. Pictured with Polly (L–R) are mechanic Don Smith and garage owner Zeke Jones. Photo Credit: Bob Bell.

GETTING OFF THE GROUND—TIPS FOR NEW BUSINESSES

If you haven't rung up the first sale on the cash register, or better yet, if your place of business isn't even built, you can put some public relations efforts to work to be sure people know about you when you open your doors. In order to presell the community (your future customers), take advantage of four news opportunities: the construction announcement; the ground-breaking ceremony; the announcement of the manager, president, or staff, or a "personality" feature story on any of the above; and the store opening.

For the construction release, send details and a photo or copy of the rendering (drawing) of the building at least two weeks prior to the ground breaking. Be sure to include details of your business operation. Releases can be sent to the business editor of the newpaper, or the architecture editor (if there is one), the news directors at radio and TV stations, and the editors of all appropriate trade publications.

Your ground-breaking ceremony should be held just before construction begins. As you want press coverage of this event, plan to have it between 9 A.M. and noon on Tuesday, Wednesday, or Thursday. Here are some people to invite:

The Mayor or representative
Members of the City Council
Planning & Zoning Commission Members

Chamber of Commerce President or representative
Presidents of civic organizations such as Rotary, Kiwanis, and
    Lions
Owners and managers of other neighboring businesses
Major suppliers
Your contractor and architect
Your banker
Your realtor

Have invitations printed on good stock (plan 5–8 days for the printing) and mail them at least 10 days before the ceremony. Follow up with a phone call to see who's coming. Be sure to include any big names in your press release telling the media about your event.

The program should go something like this: Welcome and short remarks by you. Short remarks from contractor or architect. Remarks and a welcome to the community from a city official or civic leader. Start shoveling. It is protocol to let the mayor or another top-ranking official take the first turn at the shovel. Don't forget thank-you notes to all participants.

GRAND OPENINGS AND OTHER IN-HOUSE EVENTS.

Grand opening ceremonies should occur on Tuesday, Wednesday, or Thursday prior to the first day of business. Follow the guidelines for ground-breaking ceremonies regarding invitations and media contacts.

A program schedule might be: Opening remarks by the company owner or president; remarks and welcome by a dignitary or celebrity; ribbon cutting or other symbolic gesture; refreshments served, preferrably alcoholic.

Get out the razzle-dazzle suit. Grand openings only happen once, and it's a chance to put on the most creative show in town and have a good time in the process.

Since example is often the best teacher, here are a few illustrations of creative openings.

• The Mansion Hotel had its grand opening in conjunction with a book party for the author of a murder mystery. The releases and invitations stated, "You are invited to a murder at the Mansion." Artichokes were served in a coffin, and a murder was staged on the grand staircase.

• At A La Carte, the gourmet emporium, the press was invited to breakfast. Whenever possible, offer eats and libations. The press is always more responsive when there is food involved.

• Although this wasn't done, here's a clever idea that was suggested for a jewelry store. The opening would be a 24 Carat Affair. Press invitations would be sent in flower boxes (the kind that long stem roses come in) and inside would be 24 carrots.

• The press party to kick off a local publisher's new list of books was, literally, a pig-out. One of the books was poetry and contained a number of pig paintings and references to things porcine. The hosts served pigs-in-a-blanket, pork pot pies, pork buns, and so on. The invitations were little pink paper pigs. Guests would include famous "porcophiles."

• A new bank opened in a small town. Actually it was just taking over another bank that had been there for some time. All the people who had accounts, plus the town's elected officials, were invited to "have a drink with your banker," which gave folks the unique opportunity to chat informally with the new tellers and managers. Not only did the event make the news, but it created goodwill in the community.

• For a store that was to sell "treasures from the Orient," the creative consultant convinced the owners to have an oriental rug painted on the surface of the parking lot. A classic Rolls Royce was the first to park on the unique car-pet. The owner was a collector and loved to have his car seen in public. Hot sake was served to the press, and the store was christened by breaking a bottle of sake against the wall.

• A publicity stunt in connection with the opening of a new restaurant turned into one of the best parties in town. While having nothing whatsoever to do with the decor or the menu of the Orient Express restaurant, a local PR firm created a New

York City Reunion Party. Admission was free if you could name the subway that went to Coney Island. Food vendors sold knishes and Nathan's hot dogs and egg creams. There was a contest for the best New York accent. Among the judges were a columnist for the paper, a radio talk show host, a TV anchorman, and a DJ—all transplanted New Yorkers. You can bet they wrote and talked about the event days before it happened, creating free pre—publicity. And with not one line of paid advertising, 3000 people jammed into that restaurant and many thousands more heard about it or read about it in the news the next day.

Create more razzle dazzle for other in-store events. Maybe you have a friend who is a sword swallower or a karate expert, or who trains lizards. Maybe they'd like to show off at your place of business. In this case, you have the makings of an in-store event, one that will suck people in just for the sheer entertainment value.

Special invitations can be sent to your friends and best customers. (Do you have a mailing list? If not, should should start one now.) You can produce those annoying but effective flyers that get put on car windshields. You can also ask your entertainment person to post the same flyers around his or her favorite haunts and give them out to other acquaintances. If your event might amuse children, put a flyer in the children's section of your local library. Use your imagination. Think about where you've seen flyers that have captured *your* attention. Tell the press in advance. Sunday's are usually good days to have kooky events, or lunch hours on business days if you are located downtown.

If you've got a gimmick, you don't need a performer. One enterprising restauranteur bought 100 Mickey Mouse hats at a rummage sale. (You know, the official kind with the big ears). He bought them because he was a funny guy and just couldn't refuse. But now what to do with them? Have a Mickey Mouse Lunch, of course. Everyone who came into the restaurant was offered the ears. If they wore them, a free drink would be served with the meal. It was hilarious. Many friends and solid return customers were made that day because everyone had such a good time. The local columnist was called and he ran an item the next day about the event.

Those are the basics. The zanier the event, the more likely the press is to come out to cover it. Bring out the tap-dancing swans, rent a clown, turn on the bubble machine, and let the music play—not just for the press, but for friends, guests, and for all the people you'd like to do business with.

EXAMPLES OF PRESS MATERIALS

For projects discussed in previous chapter.

FOR IMMEDIATE RELEASE

CONTACT: Toni Delacorte
OR: Patty Hudson

GRANNY GOOSE TO THE RESCUE

TIBURON, CALIF., July 29—Granny Goose, famed "spokes Goose", Granny Goose Foods Inc. is on the scene today here in Tiburon with the Marin Humane Society to return Goosey, the blind goose, to her natural habitat.

Last week, Goosey and her feathered friend and companion, known as her "seeing eye goose", roamed the area together, until a recently identified party took her friend and is believed to have "cooked his goose" for dinner.

While the District Attorney is investigating, Granny Goose is contributing $500. in memory of the deceased goose for the benefit of Goosey and other abused animals helped by the Humane Society.

Because the Marin Humane Society must rely on contributions to further their cause—up-keep of the Society, investigating cases of neglect and caring for endangered animals, Granny Goose hopes her gift will encourage others to also help the Society in it's work.

PHOTO STORY   CONTACT: Toni Delacorte
GRANNY GOOSE   FOR IMMEDIATE RELEASE
GETS GOLDEN EGG

    Granny, the mascot of Granny Goose Foods, Oakland Calif. is pictured here receiving the "Golden Egg Award" from the Marin Human Society. Granny came to the rescue of "Goosey" a blind goose who was in trouble after her seeing eye goose mate was killed. Granny donated $500 to the Marin Humane Society in memory of the slain goose and in recognition of work the Society did to investigate the unfortunate incident. Because the Humane Society must rely on contributions for their up-keep, investigations of cases of neglect and caring for endangered animals, Granny Goose hoped her gift would encourage others to also support this worthy non-profit organization. With Granny, (L-R) are Earle Ingalls, brand manager of Granny Goose and Rick Johnson of the Marin Humane Society. The Golden Egg has an accompanying plaque which reads: To Granny Goose in recognition of their concern for all animals and for their kind contribution to the Marin Humane Society, September 29, 1980.

September 26, 1980

NOTIFICATION OF
PRESS CONFERENCE: Contact: Toni Delacorte
MONDAY, AUGUST 13, 10:00AM
2220 SACRAMENTO STREET

CITY BUREAUCRATS THREATEN TO SHUT DOWN SF'S HISTORIC MANSION HOTEL: THEY WANT A ROOMING HOUSE INSTEAD

Mansion Hotel owner Bob Pritikin will hold a press conference at 10:00AM, Monday, August 13 at the hotel, 2220 Sacramento Street, San Francisco.

For more details, please referer to attached press release.

NOTE TO EDITORS & REPORTERS: For those unable to attend the press conference, Mr. Pritikin will be available throughout the day at the Mansion for personal or telephone interviews at 929-9444. In addition, District Attorney Joseph Freitas will also be available for comment by telephone: 553-1741.

ARRESTINGLY ENTERTAINING FASHION SHOW TO HIGHLIGHT"ESCAPE FROM ALCATRAZ" GALA PREMIERE EVENING

The very latest in criminally fashionable attire will be presented by Hastings on Thursday evening, June 21 preceeding the world premiere showing of ESCAPE FROM ALCATRAZ at the Palace of Fine Arts in San Francisco.

Proceeds from the evening will benefit the Guardsmen, (a service organization with helps send underprivileged youngsters to summer camp) some of whose members will be modeling fashions related thematically to a bust out of prison.

The fashion-conscious potential escapee might consider the following: a Christian Dior robe for the night before; swim briefs for the sea route and a jogging outfit once on land; a tuxedo to eventually celebrate in.

These are but a few of the entertaining fashion vignettes and commentary which Hastings will be providing. In addition, Hastings will present a gangster fashion spoof starring KNBR radio personalities Mike Cleary, Frank Dill and Carter B. Smith.

This unique fashion show is expected to take place concurrently with dinner which is scheduled to begin at 7:00 PM. FOR MORE INFORMATION ABOUT THE GUARDSMEN BENEFIT PREMIERE OF "ESCAPE FROM ALCATRAZ" AND THE GALA EVENING, CALL 781-6785. (Press reservations should be made through Toni Delacorte or Randi Ryan at 397-6300)

FOR IMMEDIATE
RELEASE   CONTACT: Toni Delacorte
MONDAY, AUGUST 20, 1979   Randi Ryan

HOT DOG DAY AT HASTINGS

IF YOU GET YOUR BUNS TO HASTINGS' POST
STREET STORE AT NOON ON THURSDAY, AUGUST
23, YOU'LL GET A *FREE* HOT DOG! IF YOUR NAME IS
FRANK, YOU'LL GET *TWO* FREE HOT DOGS. IN AD-
DITION, THERE WILL BE A SPECIAL PERFORMANCE
BY THE POWELL STREET JAZZ BAND PLAYING
"HOW MUCH IS THAT DOGGIE IN THE WINDOW".

FOR IMMEDIATE
RELEASE: CONTACT: Bob Pritikin
FRIDAY, MARCH 14, 1980

LETTER CAMPAIGN LAST HOPE FOR
BELEAGUERED MANSION HOTEL

On April 3 at City Hall seven San Francisco Planning Commissioners will decide the fate of Bob Pritikin's reknown Mansion Hotel.

Pritikin pins his hopes on an outpouring of letters of support from San Franciscans concerned about preserving landmark status buildings.

Acting on a hotel license issued by the City and County of San Francisco, Pritikin transformed a crumbling rooming house into a Victorian jewel of a small hotel. He filled it with antiques, murals depicting the history of San Francisco and presented an extensive collection of Bufano sculpture. The small hotel now adds nearly $30,000 each year to the city coffers in hotel taxes, where formerly there were none.

A technicality in the zoning code which permits a rooming house but not a small hotel generated the dispute which caused the City to file suit against the Mansion.

Because the Mansion Hotel has been unanimously recommended for Landmark Status by the S.F. Landmark Board, the Planning Commission now has the opportunity to grant a Conditional Use permit for Pritikin to operate.

"The landmark Mansion could fall to the wreckers ball," laments Pritikin, "because I can't maintain the enormous structure on the modest income of a rooming house."

Pritikin is urging all Mansion supporters to express their concern by writing to Toby Rosenblatt, President, SF Planning Commission, 100 Larkin St. San Francisco CA 94102.

-30-
* FOR IMPORTANT ADDITIONAL INFORMATION,

À LA CARTE, BAY AREA'S LARGEST
INTERNATIONAL GOURMET SPECIALTY STORE
TO HOST SPECIAL PRESS BREAKFAST ON
MONDAY, NOVEMBER 6

à La Carte, located at 2055 North Broadway in Walnut Creek, will host a special press breakfast on Monday, November 6 from 7:30–9:30 AM.

The breakfast is being held during the store's "Preview Week", prior to its grand opening to the public.

This event will provide the opportunity to both sample some of the extraordinary imported and domestic products in the store and to meet à La Carte's innovative proprietor, Sanford Ress.

FOR BREAKFAST

AS A SPECIAL PREVIEW OF À LA CARTE PRIOR TO ITS
GRAND OPENING. PLEASE JOIN US FOR AN INTERNATIONAL
SELECTION OF COFFEES, TEAS, CHEESES, PRESERVES,
BREADS, SMOKED SALMON, FRESH FRUIT, BAGELS, AND
AN ASSORTMENT OF OTHER DELICIOUS EYE-OPENERS:

Monday, November 6, 1978
7:30 - 9:30 AM
2055 North Broadway, Walnut Creek

THE EXTRAORDINARY WINE, LIQUOR AND GOURMET FOOD MARKET

7

POLITICAL PR: The Methedrine Bat Syndrome

The immortal Dr. Hunter S. Thompson aptly described the political scene by referring to a mythical "methedrine bat" in his book *Fear and Loathing on the Campaign Trail*. It is a singularly appropriate term. Observe the tiny bat, flapping its wings many times per minute. Imagine said bat after a hit of speed, and you have the general idea of the pacing involved in a political campaign.

The novice political publicist usually works for a candidate who is an up-and-coming young attorney whose name nobody knows. He or she works for love, not money. Which is as it should be. The first rule of the game is: Don't work for a candidate or issue you don't believe in.

This philosophy runs counter to the "hired gun" syndrome —the political pros who go to the highest bidder, regardless of party, morality, or their own better judgment. Hired guns do this because they make their living by winning, so they can't afford to lose. It hurts their reputation, and no one hires them any more. But even hired guns have to begin with the basics and earn their reputation. That's what this chapter is about.

CAMPAIGN REALITY

Because the campaign has little money, the publicist will wear many hats. In big, expensive campaigns, the publicist is the press secretary, pure and simple. However, in small campaigns, the publicist will probably end up being one of the strategists. He or she will also handle sign orders, write speeches, brochures, flyers, electronic media spots (maybe), and print ad copy. It may be necessary to do a little graphics work. It may be necessary to buy the media time or space. The role of the publicist in a small or poor campaign is usually pivotal. This position allows PR persons to develop a dangerous misconception. They begin to think they are very important people. They envision themselves hatching plots—in the proverbial smoke-filled backroom—that will devastate the opposition. They imagine tete-à-tetes with elected officials, who will be overwhelmed by their sagacity and political profundity. They envision press conferences every day, lights, camera, action, future gubernatorials, and maybe, just maybe, the presidency.

It is necessary to return to reality. Realize, first and foremost, that no campaign was ever won by press and publicity. Granted, it is one of the more important aspects of campaigning, but without good precinct work, volunteer coordination, and a variety of other musts, no campaign will win. The publicist is a cog in the wheel, not the wheel itself.

So get off Cloud nine, and get used to the grim fact that an inordinate amount of time will be spent on one's fanny in front of a typewriter, churning out page after page of thoroughly forgettable rhetoric. Hours are spent haggling with printers, photographers, graphic artists, and button makers. When the local crazy calls in, he's referred to the publicist. When the local editors call in, they are referred to the publicist. When the candidate gets lost and can't find his talk show, he's referred to the publicist.

Publicists lose sleep, their sense of humor, and quite probably their minds. Why? Because political catastrophe is always imminent. The campaign manager—who knows that you haven't slept for three days—usually announces impending disaster around 2 A.M. This means that a press conference must be put together by 9 A.M. The candidate can be expected to call around 5 A.M., wanting to know what color socks he should wear to the conference. It is justifiable to tell him to place the socks in a part of his anatomy where color coordination is of no consequence. It keeps candidates humble to be scolded occasionally.

In short, political PR people work for free in a way they never worked for money. The campaign headquarters will probably qualify for federal disaster aid by the last week of the running. The staff will be physical wrecks, because they haven't slept and have eaten nothing but junk-food-on-the-go for months. Their blood is half plasma, half black coffee; their lungs are full of gooey black junk from too many cigarettes; they have black circles under their eyes; they have black ink on their trembling hands; their speech turns the air black.

The publicist will be emotionally battered: by the press, who want to speak to the candidate regarding a touchy issue—and by the candidate, who is hiding from the press; by volunteers, who hold the publicist responsible for lousy decisions; by his or her spouse, who is suing for desertion; by the neighbors, who are tired of feeding his or her children; by the dog, who will growl and bite whenever he or she happens to make it home.

Most campaign staffers swear never to do this again. But chances are that by the end of an election, one has become a hopeless political junkie. You have found a candidate or cause that you believe in. You have found that political reporters are some of God's more interesting critters. You have made some very special friends. And, if all of this doesn't get you, winning will.

There is nothing like an election night high, when months of effort begin to take shape in the form of votes (political PR is definitely not for those seeking instant gratification). As the count slowly moves up, spirits move up with it. Everyone waits for that one precinct that will put the campaign over the top. And all hell breaks loose when it comes in, and the win is in the bag.

Campaigns also lose, of course. When the votes don't roll in, the tears roll down. People begin drifting away to other parties where the victory is more certain. Soon, only the hard core campaigners remain in the ruins of a dirty room, the glitter and glamour gone. The crepe paper and balloons look cheap and garish in the inevitable fluorescent light. The faces that looked young and fresh several months ago are now drained. Everyone wonders where things went wrong, and swears off politics forever.

Forget the losses. We all lose sometimes, even when the best campaign possible has been run. And believe me, when the next campaign rolls around, the same folks will be out there again, wiser because of past experience. Recover, and get ready for the next round. This is how to start.

REALITY IS NOT FOR REAL

Before beginning a campaign, you must understand a few basic "attitude laws." The first is: In a political situation, reality is not for real. You may *know* that the candidate is an honest, God-fearing, apple-pie-and-Mom-loving American. But if most of the people out there think your choice for City Council is a free-wheeling, free-loving, free-loading son or daughter of a bitch, you have what is commonly called a credibility problem. Congratulations, you have just met the American public. And, the sooner it is understood that it is their opinion, not the campaign staff's, that is of consequence, the better off everyone will be.

A second attitude law is: No hero worship. Campaign staffs exist to kick the candidate's behind, not kiss it. Candidates are not infallible. That's why they have campaign staffs. Candidates get weird ideas, and do weird things in the heat of a campaign. Once a candidate for City Council got it into her head to put up billboards (expensive!) that said, "These billboards will not be removed until Jane Doe is elected to the Smithburg City Council." It took her overworked and underpaid campaign manager almost two weeks to convince her that the money could be spent in a better way. Not to mention the fact that the project could have become quite expensive if she had lost in that election.

Another example of candidate fallibility involved a high visibility candidate in a statewide race. The campaign staff had just flown into the San Francisco Bay Area, and the candidate was annoyed with both the advance man and publicist because they had vetoed a part of his speech. As they headed for the car, a local flower-and-religion peddler headed for them. The publicist took the extended flower and kept walking, still arguing with the candidate who, in a sudden fit of pique, grabbed the offending peony and flung it in the face of the giver. Next, he loosed a stream of obscenities that made it perfectly clear that he was nowhere near Nirvana, nor was ever likely to be. His bellows had the entire lobby enthralled.

The staff members realized that their only hope was a bank of phone booths to the right. With great aplomb, they collared the offending mouth, unceremoniously shoved him into the nearest booth and slammed the door. He yelled. He pouted. He threatened to fire them. They told him he could, but meanwhile, they intended to do their job. Several hours later, a shamefaced and contrite candidate offered his apologies. But, he easily could have fired them. That was just a chance they had to take.

The moral is, be professional, even when you're not paid. It's your reputation on the line. The candidate is not God's gift to humanity and probably won't even save his little corner of the world, much less all of it. The publicist must create and preserve the public image, and that can't be done with something that is worshipped.

Also avoid press paranoia. In most campaigns, at least three-quarters of the staff is absolutely convinced that the press hates *their* side and loves *the other* side. The most innocuous article is considered outrageously slanted. Reporters are out to get them. If not reporters, then their editors. It often takes several campaigns to figure out that your opponents usually feel the same way.

The press is not out to get you. Remember that. Reporters in particular try to be fair. Understanding some of the laws governing media and political coverage can help dispel political paranoia. Campaigns are usually governed by state and federal laws. Check with the secretary of state in your state for the laws applicable to the campaign.

One law that most states have concerns equal time. This means that each candidate must have the same amount of time made available to them as to other candidates, be it paid or free, and in the same time slot. If John Schmoo is on a Tuesday evening 9 P.M. talk show for ten minutes, then every other candidate in that race is entitled to the same time in a similar slot. Having your candidate be put on a ten-minute talk show at 2 A.M. is *not* equal time. Many more viewers or listeners are tuned in during prime time hours than at two in the morning. So insist not only on the same amount of time, but also on an appropriate time slot.

News programming is exempt from equal time, although there are some instances where the content of a news program can be questioned and equal time obtained. But usually, news is news, and whoever makes it is the one who gets the coverage.

Federal laws are more general. The Federal Communications Commission (FCC) governs fairness in media. If you feel that a station in your area is consistently presenting biased information, or granting access to certain issues or candidates and not to others, then you should complain to the FCC, but only as a last resort.

However, try every possible avenue before filing a complaint with the FCC. Both print and electronic media are working under unnecessary restraints, which many believe to constitute an abridgement of freedom of the press. Make sure that you have a good case before you file. If you can work it out with the station, and avoid invoking the authorities, by all means do so.

While the press isn't usually out to get you, if the candidate isn't prepared properly, if deadlines are missed, if press conferences are called for no good reason, if the media is flooded reams of news releases on non-news items—don't complain when the press rakes the campaign over the coals. It's well deserved.

The last attitude law says: Campaigns are fun. Keep telling yourself this, if you want to survive. Campaign workers who refuse to have fun go crazy. Go out and get drunk with the rest of the staff (after hours, please). Sit up half the night plotting absurd strategies. Plague your nonpolitical friends with war stories. Send Aunt Maude in Peoria an autographed photo of the candidate. Hang out with the advance team—they usually have great war stories. Retain a sense of the absurd to the bitter end. It's much more valuable than a sense of humor. If you aren't having fun in a masochistic sort of way, then forget it. You aren't cut out for politics.

Once attitudes are in order, lay the groundwork for the campaign.

LAYING THE GROUNDWORK

Preparing The Candidate And The Speakers

In any good campaign, the behind-the-scenes-action begins almost a year in advance. The candidate who hits with a bombshell press conference announcing the support of half of the city's elected officials and other assorted luminaries, not to mention a war chest of several thousand dollars, has been working hard for a long time.

Be it candidate or cause, the publicist presents the case to the press and the public. With a candidate, you already have a personality. When working an issue campaign, select several people who can go out and present your side in a reasonable, coherent manner. Senior citizens, well-bred college students, and elected officials often make good political speakers. Elected officials lend credibility to a campaign, everybody loves grandmas and grandpas, and students have an unending amount of energy, once it's channeled in the right direction. Candidates should have a couple of surrogate speakers, since three events will undoubtedly be scheduled at the same time, or so close together that it will be impossible for the candidate to make them all. Candidates also get sick, but it isn't politic to offend the Tuesday Afternoon Bowling League, or the End-of-the-Month Ladies Tea Club by not having someone show. So, have a little help on hand for the candidate.

Don't get sucked in by the campaign firebrands! There are at least two or three people in every campaign who are morally self-righteous and loudmouthed, and want to go public with their afflictions. They have years of campaign experience. They know all the answers. They have all of the right connections. They know the governor and the editor of the local daily newspaper personally. They can turn out a thousand foot soldiers in one day to walk precincts. But they usually can't keep the promises they make, and even if they could, they are not the kind of people who should be out representing the campaign. Forget them, unless you want to spend all of your waking hours trying to rectify the damage done by their mouths.

Before loosing the dogs of war on the public, make sure that the candidate and speakers know and understand: *all* of the issues, and how they relate to other areas; the probable line of attack from the opposition; the nature of the vote that you are going for.

Before any press conference or public appearance, brief the speakers to make sure that they know these things. Play devil's advocate. Better that you rake them over the coals to get them prepared than having the press do it and prove that they aren't. This latter is definitely not good for the public image. This practice procedure will also weed out early on any mistakes in judgment that have been made regarding speakers. Speakers should not only know what they are going to say, they should also mold it to the occasion, and keep it within the alloted time limits. Most organizations allow each speaker three to five minutes to present their platform, and that time limit should be honored.

Once upon a humorous occasion, an endorsement luncheon was given by a local attorney's organization. Candidates for the office of County Assessor were being given three minutes to speak. The show started when a heavily accented candidate proceeded to give a fifteen-minute speech. No one stopped him, because all were thoroughly astounded by what he was saying. The gentleman was apparently proposing to audit, and one presumes, to tax prostitutes—hardly a function of the assessor. Needless to say, everyone got a good laugh except that candidate, who did not get the endorsement.

The problems with the speech were numerous. The candidate exceeded the time limit, and obviously had no grasp of what would be expected of him as county assessor. The press secretary had not worked with him to make his heavy accent understanable. (An accent can often be an asset, but it must be understandable.) Finally, it became obvious through a series of little jokes interspersed amid the campaign talk, that the candidate thought he was addressing a group of doctors instead of attorneys. This is a prime example of sloppy work. It is inexcusable, at any level of campaigning.

Once it is determined that the chosen speakers can, in fact, speak, see to it that they dress properly. If your guy has a penchant for plaid polyester suits with the crotch hovering somewhere around the kneecap, you've got problems. Likewise, women who are prone to tornado hairdos, smudgy eye makeup, and dresses with yesterday's dinner down the front will present a problem. Fortunately, sloppy personal appearance is easily remedied.

Generally speaking, all candidates should be well groomed and clean, and should avoid overpowering aftershave or perfume. Males should wear conservative suits, shirts, and ties for most occasions. In less formal circumstances, slacks and a nice sweater or sports jacket will do. Keep the colors conservative. He is running for public office, not going out for the male lead, if such a thing exists, in a Busby Berkeley extravaganza.

Like it or not, female candidates have to worry more about personal appearance than do men. Keep the hairdo and makeup simple, because she won't always have time to powder her nose or spend two hours in a hair-setting session. Consider a wig for emergencies, but make sure it's as close to the candidates own style and color as possible.

In the mid-1960s, one woman got bored with her looks about halfway through the campaign. She came toddling into headquarters one fine day with a Dolly Parton blonde wig covering her own short, dark hair. The staff finally convinced her that nobody would recognize her as a curly blonde (This is a good ploy. Candidates hate not being recognized.) and that even if they did, she would be in for a hard time, especially from snide columnists.

Choose simple, tailored suits and shirtdresses, and keep jewelry to a minimum. And for everyone's sake, don't try to become a femme fatale. Sex appeal is okay in moderate amounts for male candidates, but not for females. If the woman has a Raquel Welch figure, stifle it. If she has a Marilyn Monroe face, play it down as much as possible.

The role model should be somebody's middle-aged spinster aunt: homey, but capable.

PREPARING YOURSELF

Prepare yourself. First, find out who the voters are. Get all of the demographic information possible regarding who votes, where they vote, and what issues they respond to. Determine whether or not a particular group, such as women or students, will present a problem for your side. Put your finger on key community concerns. Pinpoint problem areas, and start thinking of ways to deal with them. Determine which issues have the broadest support.

By the end of the research, you should know exactly what percentage of the voters are male, female, black, white, Chicano, Asian, gay, under 25, over 60, or handicapped. Know the concerns of each group. This is the constituency. These are the people who must be convinced to vote for your side.

Now set up your press contacts. Call the editors of the local papers. Ask if they will be endorsing in the race, and tell them that a press kit is on its way. Get it in the mail immediately.

Compile the tools of your political PR trade, starting with a press list. With electronic media, determine whether or not there are talk shows that will deal with political subject matter. Finally, obtain information on preferred format and deadlines.

Don't miss deadlines! A publicist was once called into an assembly race late in the campaign because the candidate was getting lousy coverage. There were grumblings among the staff about sabotage from the opposing side and prejudice on the part of the local media. A few quick questions made it obvious, however, that any self-respecting saboteur would walk into that headquarters, look around, and leave. It was classic Pogo: "We have met the enemy, and he is us."

Nobody had bothered to check deadlines. Each day, reams of paper were sent to the local media with absolutely no determination of whether or not they were timely. Remember that many newspapers are computerized, and everything but the news is put to bed several days in advance. So, the Thursday news conference may be covered on Thursday with no problem, but unless the calendar announcement for the fundraiser was in by Monday, it won't run.

You may want to commit the press list to labels, since political releases are always mailed to the same people. Make sure that the names and addresses are correct. These labels will save a lot of envelope addressing in the future.

The press kit is your next concern. The first ingredient is an 8-$\times$-10, black and white, vertical head shot of the candidate. If it is an issue campaign, consider using both a vertical and a horizontal shot that captures the essence of the campaign. Next comes a biography for a candidate or a fact sheet for an issue —one page only. The last ingredient for the press kit is the candidate's statement of candidacy, or a general position paper for the issue. The statement of candidacy should tell, in the first person, why the candidate is running and what he or she hopes to accomplish. A position paper should sum up why the group is taking its stand on this particular issue. In either case, keep it short and sweet. Press kits crammed with rhetoric and ten pages of extraneous ramblings are unpopular.

If the endorsements are impressive, by all means include them in the press kit, too. Nothing lends credibility like having elected officials, leading community figures, neighborhood groups, and a smattering of the local clergy on the endorsement list. The endorsements can also indicate a wide basis of support, something the press considers second only to money in determining the most viable candidates. And the most viable candidates get the most coverage.

Before each press conference, add the appropriate release to the kit. It is also permissible to add brochures, clip sheets, or anything else you deem pertinent.

The political press kit is used for a variety of purposes. The basic kit naturally goes to all editors and reporters who will be involved in the endorsement process. It should be handed out to reporters at the announcing press conference. It should go to the presidents of any groups who will be endorsing in the race. And, it can be used by the fund-raisers to help pull in big money donations. (If people are going to throw $500 into the ring, they want to know what they are getting for their money.)

Now then. Make sure your typewriter works and that you have a spare ribbon, a lot of white-out and pencils, and several reams of cheap paper for all the rough drafts you are going to write. You're ready to go.

CONCEPTS OF THE MEDIA CAMPAIGN

First, decide with the candidate and the campaign manager what kind of a campaign to run. If the candidate is an incumbent, a low profile media campaign oriented toward news events is usually best. There are several reasons for this. As an elected official, the candidate is in a position to know what is going on in his bailiwick before others do. It is perfectly natural for officeholders to hold press conferences regarding issues of concern to their constituents. In other words, an elected official has access to more newsworthy information, and a podium to stand on, whereas his or her opponents do not.

Because the resulting coverage is in a news format, the opposition cannot demand equal time—and one thing you never want to do is provide a platform by which someone with no name recognition will be able to obtain it. Therefore, the incumbent should stay away, for the most part, from feature-type articles and talk shows. However, remember that equal time has only to be offered—if the candidate refuses, but the talk show hostess decides to go ahead with the debate anyway, reconsider the refusal.

In a situation where your candidate is running against an incumbent, do everything possible to force the incumbent into a high visibility race. Name recognition is the name of the game, and if your candidate has none, it's your job to get it for him or her. This can be done in several ways. Challenges to debates are usually worthwhile, as are leaks to the local political or popular columnists.

Perhaps the most important weapon available to a challenger is the incumbent's record. She has been in office for several years, and can be held accountable for her actions. Get a copy of her voting record and of newspaper stories regarding her stand on the issues. There will inevitably be two or three stands that are not popular with the public. Capitalize on them. They should be worked into campaign literature, and repeatedly brought up at endorsement meetings and other public appearances. Make sure the press knows about the incumbent's unpopular stand.

Unfortunately, a candidate sometimes runs against someone who has a very good record and is appealing to the same voting segment that he or she is. In this case, simply present the candidate with best foot forward.

In a recent City Council race, one of the main reasons a candidate won was that he was positive. The staff decided that the people of Oakland were tired of hearing gloom and doom preached. There were some good things about Oakland, and they decided to let people know what they were. It worked. While other candidates offered the public another dose of doomsday served up with a frown, the eventual winner walked around with a smile, saying "Hey, we've got some good things too. Let's see about making more good things happen." He didn't make promises he couldn't keep. His stand on the issues was not significantly different. But the attitude, the tone of the campaign, was. The candidate stood out like the sun, while all of the other candidates blended into a gray mass of clouds—and all just because he took a positive approach. Be sensitive to the public, to their mood. Read it right, and you've probably got a winner.

Most reporters recognize a political setup without too much trouble, and will avoid it like the plague. If you are grandstanding, be sure the facts are correct, and, if you are making accusations, you had better be able to provide substantial reasons for making them. No reporter is going to risk a lawsuit over a story with dubious origins.

DEALING WITH THE PRESS

The three major press tools in a political campaign are: the press conference or news release; feature articles and talk shows; and the local calendars and columns for announcing campaign events.

News events are good for several reasons. First, they tend to display your candidate more prominently in both print and electronic media than do feature items. News is prime time, talk shows aren't. It's that simple. News is also exempt from the equal time requirements. You can get coverage on your candidate or issue, but the opponent has no right to equal time. There are basically two types of news events for political purposes: the press conference or hard news, and the "fluff" piece, or feature-type, soft news.

PRESS CONFERENCE

The first press event should be a conference announcing the fact that your side is out there running. The conference should be held on the day the candidate files for office, or on which the proper authority says that the issue has enough signatures to be put on the ballot. The conference is usually held at the site of the filing. Timing is important. File too early, and nobody covers because there is no interest. And even if they do, people tend to forget. File too late, and you run the risk of having the candidate lost in a sea of other filing candidates. Usually, three to five days before filing closes is a good time.

The press release should state that the candidate is running, how much money is expected to be raised, what kind of campaign will be run.

The money question is touchy. Never lie to the press about how much money the campaign has. It's a matter of public record in most states. If things really look grim, simply say the campaign expects to raise enough money to cover expenses. Remember, an answer isn't required. But money is a determining factor in any campaign, and the press knows it. So handle the question carefully and well.

Be warned that these announcement conferences are fickle events. The entire press corps may turn out when Suzie Jones files for dog catcher, but only two reporters from a monthly throwaway appear when Jane Wong files for Senate. Don't get hurt feelings if turnout is low on the initial go-round. Even reporters and editors can't explain this enigma. Since nobody can explain it, you shouldn't worry about it. There will be plenty of other opportunities for coverage.

There is another reason for the first press conference. Once it's over, check your door list and plan an itinerary that encompasses every media outlet that did not appear. With the candidate in tow, hand deliver the press kits to the appropriate editors and reporters. This is good political PR for several reasons. First, the reporters covering the campaign will like the fact that the candidate himself has bothered to come by. They will have a warm body to associate with the name. Second, *you* have met the right people. The local press czars sometimes won't deign to see a mere press secretary, whereas they will see a candidate. If you just happen to be there, so much the better. Finally, you can rest assured that the press kit is in the proper hands. Remember that both editors and writers tend to lose things like press kits. More will have to be sent out, but at least the right people have met the candidate.

Don't take a lot of time. Media types are usually on deadline. Simply say that you are sorry they could not be at the conference, here's the press kit, and please call if you can do anything for them.

Please remember that the publicist is not the candidate. The media is not interested in your views on anything. Let the candidate talk. Publicists are background people, and should not be intrusive. At a meeting one time a candidate's press secretary would not let him get a word in edgewise. All of the questions were either answered directly by, or expounded upon by the press person. A subsequent news story insinuated that the candidate could not speak for himself and had no opinions of his own. So keep your mouth shut. Don't play mute, but don't operate under the misconception that the media is interested in your life story and views of the world.

Never grant an exclusive on a major news story. If the campaign uncovers graft and corruption in City Hall, and can prove it, hold a major news conference. That way everyone will be happy. All of the media will have a good story. The candidate or issue will get extensive coverage. The constituents will have their worst fears about City Hall come true, and will be able to say "I told you so."

If a story is leaked, the media outlets who were left out are going to feel left out. Exclusive coverage happens in only *one* media outlet. And future relations with members of the omitted media may be strained, at best. The time and place for a leak is discussed later.

Any news event must be carefully planned and carried through in order to succeed. The all-important rule to remember is: *Something must happen.* News is active. Opinions are not news, unless they are coming from the Supreme Court or some other entity slightly more revered than your candidate. Fundraiser parties are *not* news. Everyone is having them, and visiting bigwigs are usually present. In order to have news, the candidate or speaker has to *do* something. And you have to find the right hook, or angle, to pull in the press.

In a recent assembly campaign, a local group brought to the campaign's attention the fact that a Superior Court judge was about to release on his own recognizance (OR) a man with five outstanding counts of rape against him. The most current involved a 13-year-old girl, who was also badly beaten.

The community group wanted to hold a press conference with the candidate, denouncing the judicial system for turning criminals loose on the street. They had prepared a 15-page atrocity report for a press release. They were basically saying, "We don't think judges are nice. In our opinion, we should slap the judiciary's hand. Let's all think judges aren't nice."

The problem is: Judges not being nice just ain't news. But the case had possibilities, and the publicist began to look for a hook —and found a good one. The candidate, a woman attorney, would file as a "friend of the court" and ask that the accused rapist, because of the nature of his record, not be granted OR. Accompanying her, and also filing as friends of the court, would be representatives of various other anti-rape and women's groups.

The press conference was outrageously successful, and got the cause and the candidate three or four days of intensive coverage. Thus, the "friends of the court" angle worked, whereas the "judges aren't nice" angle didn't. (If you don't believe this story, ask any reporter if they would have covered that story.)

First of all, something was happening. A candidate for office *and* concerned citizens were filing in court to prevent an accused rapist from being released. They were successful. Within two days, people were aware of the fact that the man was in jail, and that the candidate was one of the people who had helped make the streets safe.

The issue was also of concern to a lot of people. Although society has not yet reached the millennium, it is beginning to regard rape as a crime and as a problem that society as a whole must deal with. If the hard core "she-asked-for-it" types could not be won over with the usual arguments, they certainly had to question the unusual circumstances of this incident—the rape and beating of a 13-year-old girl, a child (whose name was never made public). In short, the idea of keeping a specific rapist in jail was much more likely to win public support than a general attack on the judiciary, which is a confusing and controversial issue at best.

FEATURE ARTICLES AND TALK SHOWS

Press conference types of events don't turn up each week. That's when the fluff pieces come in. A fluff piece is a newsy feature-type story—human interest and the like. About half the time you'll get coverage, half the time you won't. Depending on the nature of the event, it may be best to invite only one television and one print reporter. Or, go for the whole bag of candy.

It depends on the event. Here are some good examples of fluff pieces that worked:

• The senatorial candidate of Irish ancestry who invited the press to make the rounds of the pubs with him on St. Patrick's Day. (Don't let your candidate drink if you try this. Nothing is worse than a drunk in front of a TV camera).

• The tap-dancing candidate, who performed his art on the steps of city hall.

• The handicapped people, who, instead of walking a precinct for a candidate, rolled a precinct in wheelchairs. Not only was it great coverage for the candidate, it was also good coverage for the handicapped.

Use your imagination. Brainstorm with other staffers and the candidate. Some of the ideas will be unusuable but funny— you'll amuse yourself if nothing else. But, you will also get a few good ones that you can act on.

Feature articles, talk shows, and similar items provide so-so coverage during a campaign. Equal time must be granted, and most stations and newspapers plan one session, or a series of sessions, for the candidates to present their ideas to the public. Do not depend on feature coverage to get your candidate or issue out there during the campaign. You have to go with news. Don't turn down feature time on principle, just realize that everyone else is using it too.

Ideas for feature stories should be worked on even before the candidate files, or the issue is ratified for the ballot because, since your side is not yet officially in the running, equal time doesn't apply.

When working with a candidate, pick two or three key issues, and begin placing him or her on talk shows and arrange interviews with local papers in order to talk about them. The public will begin to identify the candidate with those issues (make sure that they are popular) and will also begin to recognize the candidate's name.

Most issue campaigns evolve out of community concerns. Get the speakers out early, talking in generalities about what the problem is. Don't show all of your cards at once. The opposition will be watching to see what arguments are presented. Don't get into the position of having said all there is to say before the campaign even begins, and then having to defend that stand for its duration.

Keep the number of issues being discussed small, whether you are working with a candidate or an issue. People get confused if they are hit with too much. They remember some things, but not others. The idea is to form an identity, and that won't happen if the Don't Dam Wild Rivers campaign decides that it will also try to save whales, seals, and endangered weeds.

By the same token, single issue candidates can often get into trouble, unless the issue has the support of 99 percent of the population, in which case the opponent probably supports it too. One of the best single issue campaigns ever run was probably March Fong Eu's first race for California Secretary of State, with political wonder Sanford Weiner behind the scenes. The campaign became identified with one simple issue dear to the hearts of us all—pay toilets. Eu decided that pay toilets were the scourge of California, and that anyone who could never find a dime at the right time—which is almost everyone—agreed with her. Ms. Eu had her serious side as well, but the public identified her, as she puts it, as a "one-tissue candidate." She had found a subject that was a sore point with everyone, and something that could also be fairly easily solved with legislation.

CALENDARS AND COLUMNS

Calendars and columns are also political media tools. Many newspapers have a separate political calendar during elections. Others include the political items in the regular calendar. In either case, find out who you deal with and what the deadlines are. Calendars are basically a tiresome little task that must be carried through each week. Most people who attend political functions are not there because they read about it in the calendar. It's just tradition, and therefore, publicists continue to use it.

Columns, on the other hand, can be very useful. If the candidate says or does something clever, tell it to your favorite columnist. Likewise, if the opponent says something nasty or makes a faux pas, don't attack him or her personally—leak it to the local gossip-columnist. If Jane Fonda is going to be in town working for the cause, get the word out through the columns. A mention in popular columns is often better than front page coverage, because everyone reads the columns and the funnies, if nothing else. Some columnists accept tidbits over the phone. Others insist on having them in writing. Find out which method is preferred, and comply.

On the subject of leaks, suppose you have something a little more substantial than a column item, but not quite enough proof to make it press conference. Or suppose there is evidence that the opponent beats his wife and child, but the campaign doesn't want to get involved in mudslinging. Now is the time to call a friendly reporter and say, "Hey, I just heard this from a fairly reliable source. We can't follow it up, but if you are interested, here is what I've been told." Mention the fact that you are talking off the record, and be sure that the reporter honors "off the record" statements. Most do, but you sometimes hit one who doesn't.

Don't get carried away with making statements off the record. There are some things that reporters simply should not be told, under any circumstances. Use good judgment in determining what those things are.

The off-the-record leak is good because it can result in negative publicity for the opposition, and your campaign need not get involved at all. As a result, your campaign avoids mudslinging and leaving itself open to charges of attacking someone for reasons of political expediency. Besides, a charge like wife beating or graft is more credible coming from someone who is not actively running against the accused culprit.

OTHER PR TOOLS

Many small budget campaigns are beginning to use paid advertising. Since the media time or space is probably all the campaign can afford (and it isn't negotiable) the publicist will end up doing the media buy. Television spots are out. Unless it's a statewide or big city campaign, they are unaffordable and probably unnecessary.

RADIO SPOTS

Radio spots are good. One radio spot hits twice as many people as a print ad, and the cost is cheaper per hit. Spots should be kept to 30 seconds, and the candidate's name or the proposition's number or letter repeated as often as possible without sounding absurd. Try to get well-known and respected people in the community to tell the public why they are supporting the campaign. Then, if it's a candidate campaign, have the person record a spot. Record a total of three to five sports, and ask the station to play them "in rotation." This means that spots one through five are played in sequence and then repeated until the end of the time being.

A candidate usually must have his or her voice somewhere on the spot in order to qualify for political rates. This problem can usually be solved in one of two ways, if you don't want the candidate to record the entire spot. At the end, he or she can say: "Hello. This is Anne Smith. Please vote for me on April 3." This is good, because it's a repeat of the name and gives the voting date. Or the candidate can simply read the required disclaimer for the spot. A disclaimer runs at either the beginning or end of the spot, and simply tells who paid for the ad: "The following political ad is paid for by the Committee to Elect Anne Smith." Check with the local stations to make sure that the disclaimer doesn't have to be worded in any particular way. And remember that the disclaimer counts as part of the spot, and must be included in the timing.

When buying time, select the time blocks containing the largest number of listeners you would like to reach. Go to your strength. If the ballot measure supports housewives, then housewives are the people you want to remind to get out and vote. Buy time between the morning talk shows, or on any other program that a housewife is likely to listen to. Ask each radio station to send you a rate card, which simply lists the cost of the ad. Also ask for a breakdown of their listenership—all stations keep demographic data on who listens to them: how old they are, what they like, race and ethnic origins, and so on. Target the groups you must hit and buy time on the stations that the members of those groups listen to.

To record the spot, contact one of the stations where you are buying time. They will almost always provide studio time and make a master tape. Dubs, or copies of the tape, for the other stations are inexpensive to make. Remember that statistics are easily adjusted to meet a given point of view. The statistics provided by radio stations are no exception. So use a little common sense, in addition to the data from the station.

PRINT ADS

Print ads can be bought if there is extra money. In political PR, you almost always need at least a quarter of a page to make an impact, and this gets expensive. Some newspapers will accept typed copy and set it into print for no extra charge. Others require camera-ready copy, which means the campaign must find a graphic artist.

Likewise, some newspapers sell space by the column inch, and others by parts of a page. Sometimes you can haggle over placement; other times you can't. In most cases, it depends on how much money you are actually spending with the publication.

Don't let an editor or salesperson threaten the campaign. If an editor tries to highpressure a publicist into buying an ad, and then becomes abusive and rude after receiving a number of "no thank-yous" tell him to take his paper and shove it. Nobody has to take this sort of thing. An editor who would perpetrate this kind of foolishness is unscrupulous.

Basically, if the campaign uses print ads, the publicist must call every newspaper where it is to run and determine their requirements. Hopefully, the graphic artist can design something that can be used by all of them, rather than having to do separate ads for each.

BROCHURES

Brochures, or a brochure, depending on what the campaign can afford, are vital. They come in a variety of sizes, are used for a variety of purposes, and appeal to a variety of people. The one thing that all brochures should concentrate on is name recognition. If you throw a political brochure into the air and let it fall, the candidate's name or the number or letter of the proposition should jump out, no matter which way it falls. In this way, even if this political masterpiece is doomed to the garbage without being read, the voter has seen the name.

Keep the brochure simple and clear. People will not read anything with a lot of small print, nor will they tolerate confusing concepts. Reduce all issues to their lowest common denominator. Describe each point in one or two sentences. It may be difficult, but in order to be read, it's necessary.

Use a lot of photographs and leave a lot of white space on brochures. A picture can often say more than words. The photos should be active and show the candidate doing something, or they should imply something. A good "implication" photo might be one where the candidate, who is not the incumbent, is shown sitting in the City Council chambers with the "City Council" sign highly visible.

One of the best action photos on a brochure came from California's State Superintendent of Schools, Wilson Riles, Sr., when he ran his first campaign. Mr. Riles was shown standing in the door of a school, smile on his face, arms open, while a horde of school children rushed toward him. It was a warm and informative photo. Schools, children, action, and the candidate were all rolled into one succinct package.

Among the brochures that you may wish to consider for your campaign are the following:

General

This should state who the candidate is, why he or she is running, and what his or her stand on the issues is. If the candidate is married, a family photo is good for the inside. Only the candidate should be on the cover. Action photos on the inside.

Walking Piece

This is a brochure that is easily held in the hand, and that precinct walkers can use. Consider designing it to fit into a No. 11 envelope as well, so that it can be mailed. Usually, a photo of the candidate and his or her name is on the front (for issues, something that demonstrates the issue, if possible; if not, a head shot of a prominent person who is endorsing your position). Put Copy and the name on the back.

Targeted Pieces

These are usually, but not necessarily, designed as self-mailers. These deal with an issue that is of concern only to a portion of the voters. For example, if a pipeline with highly flammable liquid is running through a certain part of town, you might wish to inform the residents along the route via a targeted piece mailed into the area where the pipeline runs.

Attack Pieces

These are questionable. They smack of mudslinging, and quite often they backfire on the sender. Very few attack pieces work, and the ones that have are usually fairly mild in nature. Some notable failures include: a piece mailed out against a black, Democratic mayorial candidate, insinuating that he was a black radical—the entire community, which is basically liberal, was incensed; the candidate who tried to play both ends against the middle, mailing one item to the Democrats and another to the Republicans. Again, both sides ended up mad. The attack pieces that usually work are comparison pieces: Would you rather have this or this? This can be particularly effective against an incumbent. Find the wost picture of that person in existence, and under it, list voting stands that are particularly irksome to the general public. On the other side, put a charming photo of your lovely candidate, and offer the voters a change. If an attack piece is written, (which is not generally recommended), be *sure* of your facts, or you'll have a losing candidate and a libel suit on your hands. And, being sure isn't proving. You must *have* proof.

Back to generalities. Usually a two-color brochure will do nicely. Try to keep the paper white, or you may have some oddly colored faces in your piece. Paper weight depends on whether or not the piece must survive the U.S. mail, but in general, political brochures should be of heavy stock—they take a beating. Don't choose paper so heavy that you end up paying a fortune in postage, however, just make sure that it is substantial.

SIGNS

Signs are the best means available for getting the name to the public. They are also expensive. Order enough signs in a large size to post the major thoroughfares in the area. Then branch out from there and determine where else signs should be posted.

Window or lawn signs, (depending on where your voters live) are also good. If the constituency is basically apartment dwellers, order window signs. If they are concentrated in the suburbs, order lawn signs.

Try to find a sign company that can provide a dark background, with lettering in a bright, day-glo-type of paint. These signs are the most visible. They are unbearably ugly, but name recognition is the primary concern, not beauty. Order signs big enough to be seen, and if possible, order the weather-resistant variety.

A campaign brochure is not a piece of fine literature, and a campaign sign is not an artistic masterpiece. Don't get arty and cute. Stay away from slogans. The only thing that should go on that sign is the name, and in the case of the candidate, what he or she is running for. This is how signs should look:
Candidates:
ELECT JOHN DOE, 15TH ASSEMBLY
Issues:
NO ON PROPOSITION J

That's all. Use other methods to explain why. Signs, more than anything else, are name and position only.

BUTTONS AND BUMPER STICKERS

Buttons and bumper stickers are usually a complete waste of time. However, all campaigns insist on having them—they're probably good for staff morale, if nothing else. Buy sparingly. Pout when the campaign manager asks for more. Wait until the entire campaign staff is threatening murder and mayhem before reordering. Then, do so sparingly. Most people wear their campaign button to campaign functions, and at no other time. So the only people who are influenced by buttons are those who are already voting for your candidate. Why bother?

This chapter should provide you with a good basis on which to launch your political career. But remember, things vary from city to city, from year to year, from editor to editor. Recheck the laws, contacts, and press lists whenever you begin a campaign. Play everything by ear. Develop your political strategies based on what is happening in *your* community, not on what was described in this book.

Good luck! Try to survive.

A PRESS KIT FOR POLITICAL PUBLIC RELATIONS:
WILSON RILES, JR.

This was the basic press kit to announce a candidacy. It includes
Statement of candidacy
Press release listing endorsers
Black and white head shot
Biography
Statement of support by Mayor Wilson

FOR IMMEDIATE RELEASE CONTACT: JUDY KIMSEY
FEBRUARY 6, 1979

STATEMENT OF CANDIDACY
WILSON RILES JR.

Oakland has the potential to become one of the great cities of America. It's time to develop that potential. It's time to develop a sense of urban patriotism, to take apositive approach to solving our problems.

We have turned the corner on economic development. The City Center Project, Hong Kong USA, the expansion of the sea port and the airport, and the advent of increased trade with the East speak well for our economic future.

Oakland is no longer San Francisco's "country cousin". We have athletic teams we can be proud of, as well as an up-and-coming ballet and symphony. We can use all of these tools to help make Oakland an important urban center. As a member of Oakland's City Council, I intend to be instrumental in achieving this goal.

My experience in state and local government qualifies me for this undertaking. As Administrative Assistant to Supervisor John George, and as Chair of Congressman Ronald Dellums Executive Advisory Board, I have worked with neighborhood groups, business, and labor. I have found that many groups are under-represented. Small businesses, the neighborhoods, and citizens from all walks of life should have a voice in the decision making process. I want to work with these groups, as well as with big business and labor, to find a constructive solution to our problems.

One of the first things I will do when elected is to bring funds amounting to half of the city's budget, in the form of pension and retirement fund investments, back into our coffers. This money is currently invested outside of Oakland. It's about time for us to invest in *our* neighborhoods, *our* businesses, *our* children, *our* future.

I am pleased to have the support of elected officials such as Mayor Lionel Wilson, Council members Mary Moore and John Sutter, Assembly members Tom Bates and Bill Lockyer, Senator Nick Petris, County Recorder Rene Davidson, EBMUD Director Helen Burke, and East Bay Regional Parks Board member Harlan Kessel.

I believe in Oakland, and in the people who live here. Together, we can build a great city.

FOR IMMEDIATE RELEASE CONTACT: JUDY KIMSEY

WILSON RILES, JR., ANNOUNCES COUNCIL CANDIDACY.

DEMOCRAT WILSON RILES, JR., today announced his candidacy for the Oakland City Council. Council member Mary Moore accompanied Riles to the filing, and Mayor Lionel Wilson, an early supporter, issued a statement in the candidate's behalf.

Riles is optimistic about Oakland's future. "We have the tools to build a great urban center," he stated, citing such examples as the City Center Project, Hong Kong U.S.A., and Oakland's athletic teams, symphony, and ballet.

Riles has also pledged to bring the pension and retirement fund investments back into the city's coffers. These funds comprise almost half of the city's budget, and are currently invested elsewhere. "We must invest in our own neighborhoods, businesses, and futures, not someone else's," Riles stated.

Riles campaign has solid funding and an impressive list of endorsers, including: Mayor Lionel Wilson; Council members Mary Moore and John Sutter; Assembly members Bill Lockyer and Tom Bates; Senator Nick Petris; Supervisor John George; Congressman Ronald V. Dellums; EBMUD Director Helen Burke; County Recorder Rene Davidson; and Superintendent of Schools Wilson Riles, Sr.

"I believe in Oakland and in the people who live here," says Riles. "Together, we can build a great city."

BIOGRAPHY
WILSON RILES JR.

BORN: May 11, 1946 in Flagstaff, Arizona.

EDUCATION: C.K. McClatchy High School, Sacramento

Student Body President
Boy's State Representative

Stanford University, Palo Alto.

Athletic Scholarship
Defensive Halfback for the Cardinals
B.A. in Psychology, 1968.

University of California, Berkeley.

PhD. in Educational Psychology near completion.

FAMILY: Son of Louise and Wilson Riles Sr., State Superintendent of schools. Married Letitia Carter in 1969. They live in Oakland with their two daughters, Elizabeth, who is five, and Vanessa, who is four months.

WORK: Since 1976, Wilson has been Supervisor John George's Administrative Assistant. As Citizen's Advisory Committee Co-ordinator, Wilson is instrumental in finding solutions to a variety of problems.

Wilson worked in the educational field for two years (1974–1975) first as a math teacher at Hoover Jr. High in Oakland, and then as a program evaluator for Educational Testing Service.

173

His political career began with his participation in his father's successful campaign for State Superintendent of Schools. From 1970–73, Wilson worked for Weiner & Co., organizing campaigns for Congressmen Pete Stark and Pete McCloskey. In 1972, he managed Congressman Ron Dellum's campaign.

Wilson also spent two years with the Peace Corps in West Africa, and a summer in Harlem with Vista.

Wilson is a member of: California Association of Health Systems Agencies; Northern California Full Employment Coalition; Niagara Democratic Club; N.A.A.C.P.; Congress of Human Needs; Chairman, Executive Advisory Committee to Ron Dellums. The family attends Church of All Faiths in Oakland.

STATEMENT OF MAYOR LIONEL J. WILSON
February 6, 1979

I am pleased to accept the Honorary Chairmanship of the campaign for WILSON RILES, JR. for the City Council of Oakland.

I watched the progress of Mr. Riles over the years and have recently had lengthy discussions with him regarding the development of our City and the hurdles which must necessarily be overcome.

I have found Wilson Riles, Jr. to be an intelligent, thoughtful and imaginative person who not only understands the City's needs but has a sound and balanced approach towards accomplishing a resolution of those problems.

It is therefore with a great deal of enthusiasm that I announce my endorsement and support of the candidacy of Wilson Riles, Jr.

LIONEL J. WILSON
Mayor of Oakland

8

Publicity for Benefits and Fundraisers: Dracula Goes to Heaven for the March of Dimes

(*BUSINESS PEOPLE:* don't skip this chapter—we'll tell you how you can cash in on some free publicity for a modest investment)

Benefits, as the name implies, benefit something, usually a nonprofit organization that relies on donations for its very existence. The immediate benefit, obviously, is cash, which is often desperately needed. There is also another benefit, good publicity, which is too often overlooked. There are plenty of books and resource material around that will tell you how to raise money. This chapter, however, is meant to help you get the most PR for your money.

A lot of organizations spend a lot of wasted time and energy sending letters to big-name stars like Joan Baez asking them to do a benefit concert for their worthy cause. While big rock concerts can raise tons of dollars, performers receive thousands of requests each year, and harried managers often don't even respond to queries. The best advice is to concentrate on local resources and talent.

Realizing a successful benefit requires a lot of time, energy, and organization. A major extravaganza should not be attempted without professional help in production. There have been too many horror stories of events that became disasters because someone forgot about security or charged too much for admission or rented a place that was too big or too small or failed to get the proper permits. This is not to say that benefits cannot be produced or promoted by first-timers. The neat thing about a benefit is that volunteers come out of the woodwork to help, especially if the event is unique and wonderful, and the money raised will be spent for something worthwhile.

There are a few general considerations that must be met in order to ensure a successful event: a ridiculously long lead time; a realistic budget (stick to it!); a targeted prospective; audience; and a creative promotional campaign.

For starters, consider this laundry list of fund-raising events;

Antique Show/Art Fair	Walk-a-Thon
Telethon	Concert
Carnival	Theater Party
Las Vegas Casino Night	Celebrity Lecture
Fashion Show	Craft Sale/Bazaar
Dinner	International Food Fest
Ball/Cotillion	Celebrity Softball/Basketball
Auction	Evening Boat Cruise
Theater/Movie Premiere	Dance Party
Golf/Tennis/Backgammon Tournament	Wine Tastings

While the main purpose of a benefit is to raise money, an effective publicity campaign will go a long way toward creating a good public image for an organization, and may pave the way for future fund-raising efforts. As a nonprofit organization, free time is available on radio and TV stations to promote the event and to throw in a good word or two about the organization. This "free publicity" concept can be used also to attract commercial sponsors who want to reap the "benefit" of some good PR for themselves.

Most fund-raising efforts require up-front money—money for rental of space, poster production, postage, and so on. Many good ideas have been squelched for lack of front money. How is it acquired? How about contacting, let's say, a car dealership or a local department store? They might well be delighted to advance the $100 to $1000 in preproduction costs or to donate merchandise to be auctioned or given away, in return for mention in print and on the air of their connection to a charitable event.

Because of the free public service time that non-profit organizations can get on radio and television, businesses can plug into this kind of publicity by creating an event which will involve or benefit one of these groups. The following is a good example:

DRACULA GOES TO HEAVEN FOR THE MARCH OF DIMES

We were asked to come up with an idea for a fall promotion for one of our clients, Hastings Clothing Stores, a northern California chain. Since Halloweeen happenings are always fun, we decided to do a fashion show followed by a Bay Area premier of a horror film. Models would wear scary masks or makeup in addition to their Hastings clothes, and the store would donate the proceeds to a local charity.

As scary movies, particularly those with vampire themes, were the current rage, we thought about renting prints of some old classics. The project was almost shelved when, after speaking with a number of theater managers, we were told that we'd have to pay them an average night's cash box receipts to rent the theater and show the film. In order to make enough money to pay for the rental of the films, meet publicity costs, and donate something substantial to the charity, ticket prices would have to have been between $10 and $20. Couldn't imagine anyone who'd want to spend that much to see old Dracula films —even with a fashion show thrown in.

We lucked out. It just so happened that a theater was planning to open a new Twentieth-Century Fox release, *Nosferatu: The Vampyre,* just before Halloween. They liked our concept and suggested we have our event as a special midnight preview on a Friday night. (The film wouldn't open until the following week.)

A lesson learned and some advice to pass on: If an event is to be in a theater (movie or stage), consider the possibility of having it at a time when the theater is "dark"—Monday nights for legitimate theater, afternoons or midnight for movie houses.

The Castro Theater was perfect. Located in the heart of San Francisco's gay community, we knew we could get a big audience for a midnight preview of a vampire film. In addition, the Castro had an organ, the perfect musical accompaniment for a spooky fashion show. (Remember, fashion shows must have music).

We wanted very much to have the event be a benefit for a local blood bank (the press could have had a lot of fun with that!) Unfortunately, the blood bank declined. They thought an association with Dracula might discourage potential blood donors. So we called up the PR person at the local chapter of the March of Dimes. They were overjoyed at the prospect of being the beneficiary of the fund-raiser, especially since their traditional fall event, "The Haunted House" wasn't happening this year.

Now that we had the film, the theater, and a charity, we needed to let people know that *Nosferatu: The Vampyre* would be shown at a special midnight preview along with an unusual fashion show presented by Hastings entitled "Sanguine Fashions for Midnight Occasions." (Clever titles for events are useful for capturing the attention of the press as well as the public.) For starters, we enlisted the cooperation of two vampire fans, whose unique talents helped us spread the word.

One of the wonderful people associated with this event was Steve Hoston, a DJ who was the March of Dimes's Dracula for their Haunted House. He had a cape and fangs and a marvellous "Gooooood eeeevening." He would be our Master of Ceremonies. He would also stroll along Castro Street in full regalia, several nights before the show, handing out leaflets and taking tiny nips in necks.

Another was Leonard Wolf, a professor at SF State University, who happened to be the country's leading Dracula expert. He has a coffin in his office. He had just come back from a promotional tour for his new book—even did the Johnny Carson Show. He was hot. He was also cooperative. We asked him if he would appear on some local talk shows and mention our event while he was discussing his book with the interviewer. He was on five television and eight radio shows. Hastings loved the free publicity, so did the March of Dimes, so did the Castro Theater, so did Leonard Wolf.

Then there was Twentieth-Century Fox. The head of their promotion department was very pleased to hear we would be doing advance publicity for them. They gave us the movie print for free since the event was a benefit. They also sent us press kits, photo stills of the movie, and thousands of slick, four-color miniature versions of the poster (they are called "heralds"). This saved us a lot of money on printing. We had only to take the flyers to the printer and have the information about our event added. We added "admit one" to about a thousand of them, cut them up and used them as tickets.

Along with BASS (a local ticket agency), the March of Dimes office and Hastings stores became ticket outlets. This afforded us the opportunity for some in-store promotion, such as displaying the flyers and vampire paraphernalia both in the store and in the windows.

We also cleverly made the price of admission a dollar less if purchased in advance. This got quite a few people into Hastings. Maybe they bought a suit while they were there. That was the whole idea—turning publicity into sales.

What about models? Good question. Hired professionals would have been too costly. We knew volunteers from the March of Dimes would not be able do justice to an Yves St. Laurent tuxedo. Hastings' image was at stake. So we schemed up a plan to get people with at least some modeling experience to participate for free.

We issued a "casting call" to be held at a spendid bar/restaurant called Heaven. In return for the promise of good publicity, Heaven paid for the printing and postage of special announcements that we sent to all the modeling agencies and schools in town. We also put up the announcements at Hastings, in the windows of a few cooperative merchants in the neighborhood, and at the Castro Theater.

The press liked the idea of naming our casting call "Dracula Goes to Heaven"—the fashion editors mentioned the event in their columns and calendars. Several radio stations ran public service announcements.

"Dracula Goes to Heaven" was sensational. Hundreds of people showed up that night to try out—some in capes and foot-long fingernails, some with ghoulish makeup. The news media loved it. All four local TV stations were there, took pictures, and ran the story on the 11 P.M. news. Two ran it again the next day at 6 P.M. It cost Heaven $100 for the graphics, the printing, and the postage. In return, they got thousands of dollars worth of free advertising—not to mention the brisk bar business they did that night.

Fifteen volunteers were selected to be in our fashion show. All had some modeling experience and all were excited about being involved in the event. All we needed now was a cheap way to get some high quality Halloween masks.

Our search led us to yet another promotional opportunity. The Don Post Studios, a special effects outfit in Hollywood who created the mask and did the makeup for the *Nosferatu* film, were contacted about two weeks prior to the event. They too loved the idea—so much so that they not only donated a dozen full-head rubber masks (worth $30–$50 each), they also sent their makeup specialist to San Francisco for the show. They even donated an exact replica of the Dracula mask worn in the film (worth about $300) to be auctioned off at the benefit. The mask was a big hit, and because of it, the March of Dimes raised an additional $435.

Don Post, among other wonders, also created the bodies for the movie *Coma.* On very short notice, we managed to get them and the *Nosferatu* mask on "Creature Features"—a popular local TV show—for a five-minute interview between horror films. A good idea for a news story and a quick phone call to a weekend assignment editor at one of the TV stations got a reporter and cameraman out to cover the makeup artist creating the effect of a black eye and a broken nose in 60 seconds. It was a slow news day. (This means not much was going on. Since it's often like that on Sunday, it's a good day to get that extra bit of coverage if you can come up with a humorous or human interest angle.) The reporter explained to her viewers that Don Post Studios was in town to help out on the fashion show that Hastings was presenting. More free publicity.

Despite the fact that we had scored a great deal of this free publicity, the advance ticket sales were not tremendous. There was a light drizzle the night of the big event. The models were in the balcony putting on their werewolf, vampire, devil, and monster masks; the March of Dimes people were pacing nervously about. And then the magic happened. People started lining up—hundreds of people. By the time the house lights dimmed and the fabulous organ started its eerie thunder, nearly every seat was taken.

Close to 1000 people were treated to an absolutely outrageous fashion show. The film, as it turned out, was not great. But it was definitely a memorable evening for everyone. Hastings, Heaven, Leonard Wolf, and Don Post got publicity for their respective stores, restaurant, book, and masks. The March of Dimes got $3000. It was a benefit that indeed benefited everybody.

How we did it—A Time Table and Summary of Activities:

Week of Sept. 3—	Concept developed and approved by Hastings; theater found; date set.
10—	Twentieth-Century Fox contacted; flyers and press kits arrive; March of Dimes and Leonard Wolf are contacted; budget & promotion strategy are worked out.
17—	Press releases, calendar announcements & PSAs are written; ticket agency contacted; flyers & tickets printed; "Casting call" idea discussed with Heaven; details and date set; casting call leaflet is designed & printed.
24—	Releases & announcements sent to all film editors, calendars & datebooks,

fashion editors, various special media contacts; photo still from film sent where appropriate; 30 & 60 second PSAs sent to Public Service Directors of radio & TV; letters sent to Public Affairs contacts & talk show producers asking them to interview Leonard Wolf.

Oct. 3— Wolf interviews scheduled; Casting Call leaflet sent to modeling agencies & posted; flyers on main event distributed at theaters; Hastings begins in-store displays.

8— Dracula Goes To Heaven news releases sent to news media; Heaven event takes place & gets good coverage; Wolf does interviews & talk shows; more flyers passed out including midnight shows at all theaters.

15— Don Post in town for some interviews & news coverage; masks arrive; Dracula leaflets Castro street late at night; news media are phoned; press tickets are sent; previously taped Wolf interviews are aired; dress rehearsal.

19— The Big Night!

Included at the end of the chapter are the press releases and calendar announcements that were used. Note the bat on the stationery. Delacorte & Kimsey stationery was not originally printed with a bat. There was a nice bat in Leonard Wolf's book that we cut out and had printed on the stationery along with the releases. Whenever possible, do something distinctive with your written materials. It's often a small, creative touch that sets your release off from the hundreds of others that arrive on the same day. When we called the Public Service Directors to see if our PSAs were being used, they all remembered the "bat release."

THE ARMADILLO BALL AND MISCELLANEOUS SPECIALS

If your organization is fairly large (over 800), theme dance parties are good fund-raisers. Local bands, just starting out, might well agree to do a benefit just for the publicity or at least give you a discount.

San Francisco night clubs allow organizations to use their facilities on "dark" nights, nights when the club is normally closed, like Monday. Sometimes there will be a rare open date on a weekend. But clubs generally want a cut for the light and sound people, as well as the profits from the bar (remember, they are in business to make money, not to do good deeds).

The Bergman/Ramirez Defense Fund needed to raise money for the legal defense of two reporters who were being sued for libel (they charged police corruption during a Chinatown murder case). Under the auspices of Media Alliance, a nonprofit organization of people who work in media-related fields, we planned the "Armadillo Ball: A Texas Rock n' Roll Party." Through a DJ contact, we located two local bands (both including several Texans among their number) who were willing to play cheap for the cause. We found a good club that was willing to give us a Sunday night for "cost" and bar profits. Now all we had to do was get people to come.

A dance party is likely to attract people who know each other. Thus, good internal promotion is essential. This means informing members of your organization via the newsletter and coercing them into selling tickets to their friends. Tickets can also be sold through ticket agencies (the club should already have a contract with them, so you won't have to pay a fee). In addition, most clubs have advertising contracts with the newspapers. Make sure your is event is listed. Check with the club's

PR or advertising person. Don't forget to include that the price of admission is tax-deductible.

Press releases should be sent to all the entertainment editors, the calendar editors for print and broadcast media, and to those particular writers who review live shows. Don't forget any reporters who have given you good coverage in the past—you might want to send them a complimentary ticket with the press release.

Flyers should be widely circulated to all affiliated interest groups (for the Ball, we had our flyers posted in all the news-rooms in town). To help make sure a flyer is actually posted, try writing "please post" or address the flyer "ATTN: BULLE-TIN BOARD."

Because this is a benefit, consider writing personal letters to radio personalities (DJs) telling them about your event and how important it would be if they could mention it on the air. If the band has made a record, a sympathetic DJ could promote the event in the following manner: "Hey, that was the Hoo Doo Rhythm Devils. If you want to see them rock out in person, check out the Armadillo Ball—a special benefit Media Alliance is throwing over at the Old Waldorf next week."

OTHER WAYS TO PROMOTE A MUSICAL EVENT

1. Call the record company that handles the band—the company may have some ideas or provide money for promotion.

2. Call the agent—find out if the band or any of its members might be available for interviews in advance of the show, or if they might be willing to do a publicity stunt: like a drum solo on a busy corner downtown at the noon hour, or an impromptu concert during a break at the Chamber of Commerce meeting (be sure to let the press know!). Some radio stations have for-mats that allow guests to chat live with the DJ. If your band can't be in town before the event, try arranging a phone conver-sation with the on-air person, either live or taped and aired later (maybe more than once).

3. Find a friendly DJ, public affairs person, or engineer at a

radio station to help you produce a PSA with music. Make the spots in 30- and 60-second lengths and distribute them to other radio stations. (Don't forget the impassioned cover letter about the wonderful things your organization can or will do with the money you raise.)

Single out one radio station to be affiliated with your event. Thus it becomes "KSAN AND MEDIA ALLIANCE PRESENT: THE CHOSEN ONES" For this to work, invite a DJ from the station to be the MC or to judge the dance contest. DJs have big egos and love opportunities to be seen in public. Don't forget to check with the PR person at the radio station.

RAISING MORE MONEY WHILE YOU'VE GOT 'EM ALL IN ONE ROOM

Although this chapter focuses on the promotion of events, the following are a few pointers that can produce even more money at a benefit.

Bands take breaks. (Remember that when you're planning the evening.) Now that you've got a captive audience, you can grab the mike and tell people about what great things your organization is doing and why it needs the money. Better yet, have the guest DJ make the pitch. Passing the hat on the spot is good. Have your hat-passing volunteers organized in advance and make sure you've got some supporters in the crowd you can count on to make the first donations. Bring the house lights up a bit so that people will be more likely to put something in the hat when it comes by.

Have literature tables and money cans by the door as people come and go. Sell T-shirts or records (maybe the record company will give you a nice cut).

Have a raffle or auction. Merchandise can be procured from local merchants (wineries are usually good bets). If the prize is especially valuable, raffle tickets can be sold at the door. Don't forget to include the merchants' names and the value of the prizes in your prepublicity (that's why they are giving you the item(s). And give the merchants a receipt, so they can deduct the donations' values from their taxes.

186

GENERAL ADVICE IN PUBLICIZING A MAJOR ENTERTAINMENT FUND-RAISER

If Linda Ronstadt agrees to do a fund-raiser, get a professional concert promoter. Publicity for concerts by artists with a slightly smaller draw, however, can be handled by a relative novice. Here are some guidelines:

★ Have a very good idea of who will come to the concert, and concentrate your publicity efforts on media outlets that cater to that potential audience.

★ Contact people who will help get the word out. Personal contacts with the news media may mean the difference between whether the event is really covered or just treated like any other news article. Start months in advance to contact everyone who might be helpful. Tell them about the event, what the organization does, and what the money will be used for. Specifically, contact: *Radio:* DJs, Public Service Directors, newspeople, and talk show producers or hosts

Television: sympathetic reporters who may have done previous stories on the organization, Public Affairs people and talk show producers/hosts (Talk shows should be scheduled as far in advance as possible for maximum prepublicity, and should air as close to the date of the show as possible for immediacy. If you can't get one of the performers, try to book a spokesperson from the organization.)

Print: music or entertainment editor, news reporters, columnists

★ Magazines have two-month lead times. Don't forget to send photos along with releases. Don't overlook college papers and special interest or "alternative" publications, and make good use of any other interest-affiliated group's publication, newsletter, or newspaper.

CREATIVE IDEAS FOR BENEFITS

People don't like to part with their money. Although boring political fund-raising dinners with standard cold chicken and cold peas seem to have become a tradition, originality does pay off. Here are a few as yet unproduced ideas for benefits or fund-raisers.

WINE FESTIVAL

(Or any liquid or product indigenous to your geographical area). A California Wine Festival, for example, would be designed to promote California wines in a unique and exciting way. More than just another wine tasting, the festival would celebrate wine in the traditional European style, allowing people freedom to enjoy wine in an outdoor setting with the interesting addition of a variety of international foods and music. The festival could be a highly original entertainment form, allowing people to experience wine as a complement to foods of other nations without having to travel long distances between wineries. Small groups of roving folk musicians would play in a rambling wooded setting. No admission charge— rather chits would be sold that would be redeemable for a glass of wine. Proceeds from the event would be donated to a charitable cause. Wineries would be charged a fee for participating to cover the cost of production, promotion, and advertising. This could be a *big* event. Held three days over a long weekend, the cost for advertising and promotion could run as much as $5000. but it also has the potential of raising *big* money if it were done with a great deal of flair and teriffic organization.

CELEBRITY BOWLING TOURNAMENT

This could be a lot of laughs. You could round up city officials, radio and TV personalities, and well-known businesses and community leader types. Make outrageous bowling shirts. Get local merchants to donate prizes. The news media would cover this one for sure! The fund-raising aspect would be to charge businesses, banks, corporations, publishers, and everyone else, to sponsor a team (their name emblazoned on the back of the shirt). The publicity they'd receive would be worth much much more than their investment.

SYMPHONY SAIL

Your city most likely has a symphony, an opera company, or other musical enitity that relies on public support. Now, if your city is also located on or near a body of water, you could organize a symphony sail—along with a fashion show from one or more of your local department stores or boutiques. Perhaps make it a black tie affair. In addition to the regular calendar and news media, make use of society editors and columnists, and museum and other arts organizations' newsletters. Boat rentals can be expensive, but it's amazing the kind of cooperation and/or discounts you can wangle if it's all for a good cause.

FASHIONS FOR LIFE—THE ALCATRAZ BASH

We staged a real one-of-a-kind wingding on Alcatraz, Island, former site of a federal prison. While it was enormously successful and got a huge amount of press, we'd never do it again. The concept was relatively simple, one that is recommended as the basis for a "different" fund-raiser: a fashion show with all the models being either police, DAs, or sheriffs. Our event benefited the Police Athletic League (summer sports programs for kids).

Because of its unusual location, we faced giant problems turning the abandoned federal prison into a glamorous nightspot. To pull it off, we used a flotilla of water craft (barges, ferries, fishing boats) and a helicopter. We also had a lot of great volunteers.

It took months of planning and the cooperation of hundreds of people to put together a party and fashion show on an island that has no electricity, no water, and only one small jeep for transportation up the hill to the main cell block, where the shindig was put on. The obstacles were enormous: how to get

400 chairs, 2 portable toilets, 10 racks of clothes, food and drink for all the guests, three heavy generators, a staging area and ramp for the models, a ton of ice and a sound system with speakers as large as refrigerators across the Bay and half a mile up the hill.

The day before the event, a group of very nervous people who were helping set up stood by the lighthouse on top of the hill at Alcatraz and watched a helicopter dangling a port—o-potty slowly move into position above the entrance to the main cell block. Despite dangerous swirling winds, the pilot made seven more perfect deliveries of most of the heavy stuff.

Meanwhile, down at the Alcatraz loading dock, a crew from the St. Francis Hotel catering staff was unloading wine glasses, chafing dishes, silver candelabras, cases of wine, linens, buffet tables, and other serving equipment from a boat. All of it was loaded into hotel linen baskets, which were then hooked up like a miniature train, and pulled up the hill behind the jeep.

We charged $100 per person and got nearly 400 paying guests. Everyone who came was totally flipped out and we raised quite a bit of money for PAL. And while the production hassles nearly qualified many of us for permanent residency in a loony bin, the promotion of the event was great fun, and the resulting publicity was fabulous.

The following is the transcript of a public service announcement produced by a friend at one of the radio stations. A number of other stations used this PSA—another example of how originality and humor really helps get the word out.

HI, DIS IS AL FROM PAL—YOU KNOW, THE POLICE ACTIVITIES LEAGUE. EACH YEAR WE HELP 5,000 KIDS IN SAN FRANCISCO BY GETTING DEM OFF DA STREETS AND INTO DA BALL PARKS. DIS YEAR IS OUR 20th ANNIVERSARY AN WE'RE GONNA HAVE A PARTY, GUESS WHERE? ALCATRAZ—YOU KNOW DA PRISON WHERE DAY USED TO PUT BAD GUYS AWAY FOR A LONG TIME. WELL NOW WE'RE GETTIN DA POLICE AND DA SHERIFF AND DA DISTRICT AT-TORNEY TOGETHER TO HELP US CELEBRATE. AND

YOU KNOW WHO ELSE? WELL, WORLD FAMOUS DE-
SIGNERS LIKE PIERRE CARDIN, HALSTON, BILL
BLASS AND OTHER FANCY GUYS LIKE DAT. THEY
GOT ALL THESE FANTASTIC CLOTHES DAT NO ONE
HAS SEEN YET CUZ IT'S STUFF FOR DA FALL SEA-
SON, NOT ONLY THAT, THERE'S GONNA BE DIS IN-
CREDIBLE BUFFET SUPPER BY CANDLELIGHT IN THE
CELL BLOCK BEFORE DA SHOW. HEY, YOU CAN'T
MISS DIS ONE, FOLKS—DA ABSOLUTELY BEST
PARTY DIS TOWN HAS EVER SEEN. YA WANNA BE
THERE ON SUNDAY, MAY 20th??? IT'S EASY. JUST
CALL THE PAL OFFICE AT 567-3215 OR YOU CAN
PICK UP YOUR TICKETS AT ANY HASTINGS CLOTH-
ING STORE. IT'S ALL TAX DEDUCTIBLE FOLKS AND
IF YOU COME TO ALCATRAZ YOU MAY BE MAKING
SURE THAT A LOTTA KIDS WONT.

SAMPLE PRODUCTION AND PR CALENDAR

Suppose you decide to go for a big event, such as a concert
or other entertainment event that is scheduled for one performance in a hall seating 400 to 1000 or more people. Here is a
sample production and PR calendar that was used for a similar
event for the six-week period before the event. This is reproduced courtesy of Suzanne Locke and Kristin Leimkuhler.

Compiled by Suzanne Locke
Kristin Leinkuhler

SAMPLE PRODUCTION CALENDAR (6 WEEK)

Toni Delacorte

1st Week

PRODUCERS: DO I, II, and III Below

I. SELECT & CONFIRM ARTIST(S)
A. Commitment must be obtained *before* proceeding with other aspects of production.
B. Resources: Talent & Booking Directory, at Public Library or Bay Area Music Archives.
C. Personal Contacts: Send letter/outline of event, statement of purpose, description of organization's short and long range goals.
D. Working with Artists' manager's.

II. SELECT A DATE
A. Per Artist's confirmation of availability.
B. Factors: Venue "off" nights, Students, etc.

III. SELECT AND CONFIRM VENUE
A. Best location. (Determined by Artist's draw)
B. Union or Non-union? (TASTE)
C. Wheelchair accessable?
D. Security
E. Insurance

2nd Week

PRODUCERS: DO IV and V Below

IV. MAKE TRAVEL ARRANGEMENTS FOR ARTIST(S)

V. HIRE PRODUCTION STAFF
(Hereafter broken down into into 3 main areas of responsibility)
A. PUBLICITY AND PROMOTION (Committee, individual)
1) Begin organizing basic data for publicity
2) Contact newspapers, radio, etc for listing deadlines.
3) Choose method(s) of ticket sales and determine price. (Bass, Teletix, your org and affiliates)
4) Select and confirm poster design.
B. TECHNICAL COORDINATION (Stage and Hall Managers)
1) Begin ongoing communication with Artists Tech staff, Hall Staff, and Event Staff.
a) Obtain hall specifications
b) Obtain stage plots, and tech info needs from artist.

SAMPLE 6 WEEK PRODUCTION CALENDAR, Con't.

    2) Work with producers to evaluate and select any
necessary technical support, establish budget.
(Sound and lighting companies, crews, generators)

C. LOGISTICS AND EDUCATION COORDINATION
    1) Recruit and organize volunteer work force.
    2) Investigate permits for Booths (T shirts, buttons,
etc. and Food Concessions.)
    3) Plan literature tables.
    4) Suggest educational speakers for performance.

D. CONSULTATIVE SERVICES
    1) Legal
    2) Accounting

                  Kristin Leimkuhler
                  Toni Delacorte

4th Week

PRODUCERS: DETERMINE VIABILITY OF EVENT.

A. PUBLICITY AND PROMOTION
    1) Begin airing PSA's
    2) Continue with previous plans.

3rd Week

A. PUBLICITY AND PROMOTION
    1) Poster printing and distribution.
    2) Begin ticket sales.
    3) Follow up on previous press releases.
    4) Send out updates and additional releases.
    5) Plan a media attraction to bring widespread attention
to upcoming event.
    6) Write PSA's for radio.

193

SAMPLE 6 WEEK PRODUCTION CALENDAR, Con't.

B. TECHNICAL COORDINATION

1) Contract necessary technical support. (Sound, lights, etc.)
2) Correlate Stage plots and Hall Specs to finalize schedule and equipment needs.
3) Estimate needed Security Staff for Stage area.
4) Recruit/hire additional tech staff as needed.

C. LOGISTICS/EDUCATIONAL COORDINATION

1) Begin evaluating volunteers' skills and channelling them into appropriate positions. (Security crew, Clean-up Crew, Ushers, etc)
2) Begin coordinating booths, concessions, and information tables.

5th Week

A. PUBLICITY AND PROMOTION

1) Continue with previous plans.
2) Produce planned media attraction.

B. TECHNICAL COORDINATION

1) Finalize schedule.
2) Schedule a production meeting with staff

C. LOGISTICS/EDUCATIONAL COORDINATION

1) Continue with responsibilities from previous week.

6th Week

1) Arrangements for tickets for Artist's guests and Press.
2) Follow-ups on previous releases.
3) Radio and TV interviews: Artists, Speakers, etc.

DAY OF SHOW

1) Acts as host/ess to press, makes press kits available.
2) Supplies tickets for guests through box office.
3) Sets up Press interviews.

Kristin Leimkuhler
Toni Delacorte

194

B. TECHNICAL COORDINATION
1) Production meeting with staff:
—Artist's Tech Staff
—Stage Manager
—Hall Manager
—M.C.
—Sound and Lighting staff
2) Distribute time schedules.

1) Everything should be finalized.
2) Backstage Walk-through with Security Chief.

1) Stage Manager and Hall Manager work to keep show running on schedule, including sound/light checks, loading, meal breaks for crew, and the performance.
2) Supervises and directs security in stage area.
3) Distribution of backstage passes.

C. LOGISTICS/EDUCATIONAL COORDINATION
1) Contact and confirm medical staff. (Generally one doctor plus assistant)
2) Arrange food provisions for event staff, day of show. (1–2 meals)
3) Plan refreshments for artist's dressing rooms. (Their preference with in reason.)

1) Finalized sales of booths and food concessions.
2) Have literature, t-shirts, and buttons ready.
3) Finalize all volunteer positions.

1) Set-up and monitor booth and concessions activity.
2) Coordinate literature tables
3) Provide meals for event staff.
4) Arrange refreshments for artist.
5) Clean-up.

NOTE: BOX OFFICE STAFF SHOULD BE EXPERIENCED AND SECURITY ON DUTY BEFORE OPENING FOR TICKET SALES.

Sample Budget
Here is a sample overall budget for a benefit concert. By looking at the projection of profit on the bottom line, you can figure out in advance whether or not your event will make money.

SAMPLE OVERALL
BUDGET   Compiled by
                                  Kristin Leimkuhler
                                  Toni Delacorte
                                  Suzanne Locke

OVERALL BUDGET/BENEFIT CONCERT

1. EVENT FACILITY & OPERATIONS

Facilities & Services

2. EXHIBITION EXPENSES

Freight & Shipping
Media Materials & Equipment
Film Segment

3. BENEFIT CONCERT

Box Office
Venue
Production
Advertising
Miscellaneous
Film Segment

4. PUBLICITY

All publicity
Publicist's Salary
Reproduction
Printing Postage
Paid Advertising
Art Design & Layout
Posters
Etc.

5. TRAVEL & SUBSISTENCE

Air Transportation
Local Transportation
Subsistence & Lodging

6. ADMINISTRATIVE

Administrative expenses for duration of project including administration after event
Salaries
Office
Contracted Services

SAMPLE BUDGET   Compiled by:

Kristin Leimkuhler
Toni Delacorte
Suzanne Locke

PROPOSED BUDGET FOR EVENT/CONCERT
(CATEGORIES)

GROSS POTENTIAL (= of days × projected
attendance per day @
$____per ticket) $_____

PRODUCTION EXPENSES
  Building
    Rent $_____
    Utilities   _____
                                    $_____

  Box Office
    Advance Sale Fee   _____
    Sellers (Days of Event) _____
    Ticket Takers (" ")   _____
    Doormen & Ushers (" ") _____
                                    $_____

  Production
    Sound & Lights   _____
    Stage & Seating   _____
    Labor   _____
    Rentals: Equipment _____
                                    $_____

  Advertising   _____
                                    $_____

  Miscellaneous

199

Decorations   _____
Insurance   _____
Talent Treatment   _____
Rehearsal: # days   _____
Security   _____
Clean Up   _____
Transportation   _____
Contingencies   _____

$_____

Office Expenses + staff salaries

$_____

Travel: Hotel & Per Diem
    Expenses, # people
    @ $____ for____days

$_____

TOTAL EXPENSES $_____

NET PROFIT $_____

SAMPLE CASH
FLOW STATEMENT   Kristin Leimkuhler
                       Toni Delacorte
                       Suzanne Locke

CASH FLOW STATEMENT
May 19, 1981

CASH RECEIVED
  Total Receipts from Donations $ _____
  Total Receipts from Concert   _____
      TOTAL CASH RECEIVED $_____

CASH DISBURSED
  Contract Services   _____
  Telephone   _____
  Equipment Rental   _____
  Copying   _____
  General Supplies   _____
  Office Supplies   _____
  Travel   _____
  Postage   _____
  Accounting   _____
  Deposits (Rent & Services)   _____
  Petty Cash   _____
  License & Fee   _____
  Rent   _____
  Miscellaneous   _____
      TOTAL CASH DISBURSED $_____

NET CASH $_____

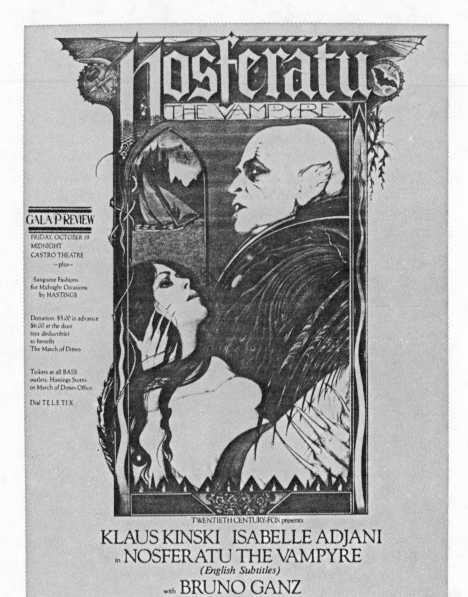

FOR RELEASE: CONTACT: Toni Delacorte
UPON RECEIPT   397-6300

SPECIAL PREVIEW OF "NOSFERATU: The Vampyre" AND "SANGUINE FASHIONS BY HASTINGS" TO BE PRESENTED FRIDAY, OCTOBER 19th AT MIDNIGHT SHOW AT CASTRO THEATRE TO BENEFIT MARCH OF DIMES

The long-awaited Werner Herzog film, "NOSFERATU: The Vampyre" will be shown on Friday, October 19th at Midnight at the Castro Theatre in San Francisco.

This special preview (the film is not scheduled to open until 10/23), has been arranged as a benefit performance for the March of Dimes.

Preceeding the film, Hastings will present a unique fashion show, "Sanguine Fashions for Midnight Occasions" . . . accompanied by the great organ at the Castro.

Tickets are $5.00 and are available thru BASS, all Hastings Stores or at the March of Dimes office. For more information, call BASS: 835-3849 or the March of Dimes: 441-1900. Contributions are tax-deductible.

ADDITIONAL INFORMATION:

Today, eighty years after novelist Bram Stoker created him, the infamous Count Dracula is experiencing an astonishing rebirth in current literature and on film. "NOSFERATU: The Vampyre" is an exciting new version of this classic tale. This 20th Century Fox release has been the hit of several international film festivals and has enjoyed a smashing success in European theatres.

203

Excellent photo opportunity

FOR IMMEDIATE
RELEASE: CONTACT: Toni Delacorte
THURSDAY, OCTOBER 11, 1979

DRACULA GOES TO HEAVEN IN SEARCH OF MODELS FOR MARCH OF DIMES BENEFIT

On Thursday, October 11, Dracula will go to Heaven (located at 1787 Union Street in San Francisco) from 9:30–11:30PM.

It is expected that hundreds of aspiring models will also be in Heaven that evening, hoping to be cast in a fashion show that will benefit the March of Dimes. Entitled "Hastings Presents: Sanguine Fashions For Midnight Occasions", this unique presentation will preceed a special preview of "NOSFERATU: The Vampyre" on Friday, October 19 at the Castro Theatre at Midnight.

Heaven's Dracula will be Steve Hoston, noted for his convincing portrayal of the vampire at the March of Dimes traditional Haunted House fund-raisers.

FOR IMMEDIATE
RELEASE   CONTACT: Toni Delacorte
FRIDAY, OCTOBER 19, 1979

HOLLYWOOD'S HOTTEST SPECIAL EFFECTS STUDIO TO CREATE MONSTERS OUT OF MODELS AT MARCH OF DIMES BENEFIT FASHION SHOW AND SPECIAL PREVIEW OF "NOSFERATU, THE VAMPYRE" FRI. OCT. 19, MIDNIGHT AT CASTRO THEATRE

On Friday, October 19 at Midnight at the Castro Theatre, a ghoulish fashion show from Hastings will precede a special preview of "NOSFERATU: The Vampyre".

The unique fashion show, "Sanguine Fashions For Midnight Occasions," will feature spectacular masks and make-up from Don Post, one of Hollywood's most creative special effects studios.

Prior to going on stage, there will be an excellent photo opportunity to shoot the models' make-up session from 10:45PM on in the mezzanine area of the balcony at the Castro.

9

HOW TO RAISE HELL FOR A CAUSE AND OTHER SINGLE ISSUE CAMPAIGNS: PR for Environmental and Consumer Groups and the Arts

You went to visit a friend's mother in a local nursing home last week, and found the conditions appalling in what is supposedly one of the better homes in your community. An elderly patient sits in a wheelchair in the hall, obviously in pain, and you overhear a nurse saying that the medication for that patient has run out, and the next delivery isn't expected until tomorrow. As you walk down the hall, several doors are open, and patients are lying in their beds naked and uncovered. You notice bedsores and bruises. When you finally reach your friend's mother, she is lying on a urine-soaked mattress, and has a bedsore that has eaten almost to the bone. Or . . . . .

You are a woman who opened her own advertising agency three years ago. You've worked your behind off making a success of your business, which is now booming. A prospective client wants to meet for lunch at one of the local business clubs. When the two of you arrive at the door, you are greeted with the fact that, although you are president of a successful business, you will not be allowed to dine in this particular club because you are a woman. Or. . . .

You have a particular passion for small furry animals, or,

large unfurred critters, say whales. You have discovered that certain species are being systematically destroyed for commercial reasons, and are in danger of becoming extinct. Or. . . .

A small but extremely talented Shakespearean Festival has been hiding out in the hills. It has been performing for seven years, and receives critical acclaim for its performances. However, it is struggling financially, and plays to half-full houses. It can't afford advertising. It needs PR.

The beastie encountered in each of these examples is a single issue, and plays to a single-issue constituency. In every case, a specific message must be delivered to a specific audience. This is where every PR person must use his or her talents to the fullest. Businesses, political campaigns, and fund-raisers all have a public relations framework that can be repeated successfully time after time. A single issue is, by definition, unique and each one is handled entirely differently. The publicist must be alert, and ready to send a news release or organize a press conference at a moment's notice. Sometimes, there isn't time to follow the usual routine. You simply grab a phone and start calling.

This chapter is going to give straight examples that will provide some concept about how to deal with a single issue. But when push comes to shove, the publicist and the organization are basically on their own.

The news conference or scheduled press event is usually a valuable tool, and may be used more here than in any other type of campaign. Each cause célèbre in the country can use some of the techniques presented here, but remember: Creativity counts.

GETTING READY

Establish the goal that must be attained, determine the quickest and easiest way to achieve it, and don't deviate unless the world comes to an end.

The goal must be crystal clear. Fortunately, it is usually

self-evident. It's the process of achieving it that is murky and, in most cases, the source of unending argument.

Before crucifying the source of the problem—the Men's Club, the nursing home, or whatever—sit down and try to work it out. They may be willing to negotiate, or they may even be unaware of the problem. A front page exposé is not always the best answer. Don't go into a meeting with murder in mind. Inside help and sympathizers are often worth a small fortune. For example, the nurse's aides in the nursing homes can become staunch allies, and the men-only club has a membership that is, by and large, sympathetic to women's rights. When the problem has no culprit—the Shakespeare Festival and whales, for example—the going is a little easier.

Don't get sidetracked. Remember the definition of single issue. Most women who have received the brunt of discrimination want to fight all discrimination. Fortunately, other groups exist who are fighting for the rights of blacks, gays, the elderly, and others. When feasible, lend your organization's name to their work. But save your group's time, energy, and money to fight its own battles.

A final word of caution. People involve themselves with an issue because something about it catches them at gut level. It often becomes their raison d'être. Keep emotions out of the public eye, however. Too many good causes go down the tubes because of emotions. The speaker gets on a local TV show and degenerates into a name-calling, foaming-at-the-mouth idiot. The organization immediately takes on a public image of having a membership consisting of fringe lunatics who are probably not adverse to bombing nursery schools to achieve their goals. Those members of the public who were on the border line are now lost, and even those who support the cause will steer clear of volunteering. Who wants to work with crazies?

Emotions also impair judgment. If you are feeling weepy, angry, or suicidal, stay out of headquarters for a few days. Retain sanity and objectivity to the bitter end.

Let's look at some single issues.

W.O.E. TO THE MEN'S CLUB

The Actors: Women Organized for Employment (W.O.E.)
The male-only Commercial Club in San Francisco. Two San Francisco Supervisors, female, one Municipal Court judge, also female. Several members of the Commercial Club, male.

The Situation: A woman who was president of her own company was not allowed to eat at the club. Many business dealings and meetings occurred here, and women were systematically denied the ability to engage in the process, to the detriment of their careers.

The Solution:

In this particular case, we had a simple, immediate achievable goal: to open up the Commercial Club to women. When W.O.E. first approached us, they had tried unsuccessfully to negotiate with the club. Although there was a great deal of support among the membership, the hardcore MCP's were preventing a vote coming to the floor on allowing women—mainly because they knew it would pass. W.O.E. had been conducting educational espionage by slipping women in the backdoors during the noon hour, and blitzing the joint with leaflets explaining their position. The response was encouraging, but, because a vote could not be taken, the situation had reached a stalemate. So they decided to go public.

The first thing that we had to do was to pull in a few women to an event that would bring out the press, and put the situation before the public in a manner that would prove so embarrassing to the club that it would have to take a vote. We had sought the advice of those club members who supported us, and they agreed that this would be a good plan.

We decided that the best way to make our point would be to have several prominent women appear for lunch, and be refused service in front of the press. The W.O.E. club membership would picket, and set up lunch tables on the sidewalk to protest the fact that they could not eat inside. In other words, the TV cameras would have something colorful and unusual to focus on. But the real cincher would have to be the prominent women —they had to have name recognition and respect within the community, and be successful in their own right. Jane Fonda would not do because she lives in Los Angeles and many people consider her too radical. Although several W.O.E. members were extremely successful professional women, they did not have the name recognition that would make the public start to wonder why somebody as obviously successful as so-and-so could not eat wherever she wanted. Phyllis Schlafly has name recognition, and respect in certain quarters, but she was not likely to agree with our cause.

We finally asked a municipal court judge and two female supervisors if they would enter the club for lunch escorted by members and businessmen who were sympathetic to the cause. They agreed.

It was also decided that the image that W.O.E. projected on the sidewalk would be especially important. We did not want to antagonize the public. We wanted to present our case in the best possible light, and not give any room for criticism in any quarter. It was agreed that everyone would wear dresses or business suits—absolutely no pant suits, much less jeans.

In doing this, we hoped to destroy the image that so many people had of feminists in the early 1970s—a bunch of bra-burning rowdies who were frustrated sexually at best, and lesbians at worst. Again, it would have been easy to say "Even though we are straight, we support gay rights, and we are fighting for them too." But it would have been a departure from our goal. That's what it means not to get sidetracked.

We arranged for each of our three prominent women to be escorted by a member of the Commercial Club who supported us. The three major points we had going in our favor were: credibility, in the form of the two supervisors and the judge; an image of feminists that would be palatable to the public at large in the form of our conservatively and well-dressed membership; and support from inside the club itself. We sent out our releases, feeling quite confident.

The confidence was well justified. The Commercial Club should have such good PR. The membership began the sidewalk setup about half an hour before the press was scheduled to arrive. We had a press table as well as our lunch tables, so that we could keep track of who arrived. The press kit included a fact sheet on W.O.E. success stories, a history of the skirmish with the Commercial Club, and the release itself. Cameras and reporters had a grand old time filming the feminist lunch-in on the sidewalk, and they were in good spirits, if not sympathetic to the cause by the time the principals arrived.

What transpired from this point on was truly gratifying. The principals entered, and were seated. French bread and water was served before the management discovered what was happening (they had been distracted by the sidewalk affair) and put an end to food service. This resulted in a wonderful headline in the newspapers: "Prominent Women Served Bread and Water at Men-Only Club." Shortly after the table was put on rations, about six more W.O.E. members, dressed to the nines in three-piece gray flannel, arrived with leaflets. And one woman reporter made our point better than we ever could have. As she interviewed two stauch misogynists at the bar, they began berating bra-burners and uppity women. Feminists were not feminine. They were scroungy and dirty, and no right thinking male would look twice at them. That's why they did all these weird things. Feminists were ugly, insecure women, and all they ever wore were jeans and T-shirts. The typical stereotype.

After listening to the tirade, the reporter simply asked: "How can you object to having lunch with these women?" as the camera flashed to our members.

As a result of this event, W.O.E. received national coverage. There was pressure from the community at large against the Commercial Club, *and* from the business community, to allow women. We had made a favorable impression. We had also forced the issue, and within two weeks, the Commercial Club had voted to let women onto the premises.

The news coverage itself was excellent. All major television stations ran us on both the 6 and 11 o'clock news. The major dailies throughout the Bay Area devoted almost full-page spreads, thanks to the number of pictures that had been taken on the sidewalk and in the club. (Lesson: Photographs get you more space. Make sure you are photogenic.) We were also covered by the wires, the *Wall Street Journal,* the *New York Times* and the *Los Angeles Times.*

A good time was had by all, we won the battle, and proceeded to focus our attention on the next bastion of male chauvinism.

JUDYS STORY:

Save The Whales—Through Education

I went to Alaska, saw my first whale, and had to be physically restrained from jumping overboard to pat it. I have since been a breast-thumping, long-winded, and ardent devotee of these wonderful marine animals. It has always escaped me why others fail to share this devotion. There were and are a number of good groups around dedicated to throwing their bodies in front of whaling ships in order to save the behemoths, and their efforts should be applauded. But it still didn't help me understand why so many people don't love whales. When I began work with General Whale, my question was suddenly answered —non-whale lovers simply don't know about whales. Anyone who knows a whale, loves a whale. General Whale exists to make sure that everybody meets a whale at least once in his or her lifetime, in one form or another. To accomplish this, the collective of artists sculpt life-sized whales, which then travel around the country with volunteers who give out information galore on the whale being displayed. This was the scenario:

The Actors: General Whale, a group of artists dedicated to informing the general public about the plight of whales.

The Goal: To introduce Pheena, GW's newest creation, to the public and start her migration around the world, amidst a great deal of brouhaha.

This was (and still is) an educational campaign to educate the public about whales. In order to do this, the artists of General Whale had obtained funding for an ambitious project—taking the would-be life-sized whales around the country, hitting shopping centers, fairs, parks—anyplace where people gather. They provide written materials to explain the mammals to the public.

The particular project, at the point where I entered the picture, was to present General Whale's new creation, Pheena the Fin Whale, to the Bay Area community, and thereby launch her migration across America. We had our literature well in hand. There is nothing like working with artists to get good-looking brochures. The materials were also well written. These idealists were practical, and had foresworn gushing and gooing and getting artsy-esoteric. They had produced solid well-written informational brochures. My job was to get press coverage for the unveiling.

One of the artists proved enterprising beyond my wildest expectations. He single-handedly arranged to have a helicopter service air-lift Pheena from her birthplace at Fort Mason to San Francisco's Marina Green. In one fell swoop, he had solved a massive transportation problem, and given us some great photographic opportunities.

We began early, by placing various artists on talk shows on both radio and television. Then, we called the major dailies and had reporters and photographers come down and watch the work in process. Many took an active interest, and would call every couple of days to see how Pheena was progressing. In other words, we had not only gotten our prepublicity stories, but we had also captured the imagination of the press. They were interested, and we knew we could get more coverage in the future.

When the releases for the unveiling went out, the press and public were invited to a birthday picnic for Pheena. Everybody met on Marina Green. We hinted in the press announcement that we had an ace up our sleeve. When curious reporters called to try and ferret out the information, we simply said "Wait and see."

The beforehand logistics on this event were a pain. First, there had been the problem of moving one-ton Pheena several hundred yards from her birthplace to the Green. And even after we got the helicopter, there were still problems. The whale had to be balanced so that the chopper could lift her. We had to have people on the ground for crowd control and to talk the pilot in. (My recurring nightmare throughout this entire project was a headline which read: "EXTRA! EXTRA! ONE-TON WHALE SCULPTURE DROPS FROM HELICOPTER, SQUISHING HUNDREDS OF SMALL CHILDREN." I'm serious. This was a real fear for me and for the rest of the crew. More work may have gone into keeping people unsquished than into sculpting the whale.) We had to have permits, written permission, oral permission, and passing nods from almost every agency within the confines of San Francisco County. The press work was the easiest part of this job. It was the background that nearly drove us all crazy. But you should be aware of the fact that these sorts of things are necessary considerations. Don't plan your parade, and forget the permit. Don't forget that your smashing idea for photographic coverage could backfire on you, if you don't plan well. Make sure that what you are doing is safe for those involved and for the public. All you need is a major mishap in front of the press to destroy your project.

We finally had the bureaucracy, the press, and the public under control. And, when Pheena the fin whale flew in and finally landed on Marina Green, we had a photographer's dream, not to mention a whale-lover's. The minute the monitors lifted the ropes, hundreds of children swarmed over Pheena, hugging her, touching her, sliding down her wonderful tail, and riding behind her magnificent fins. People were flying whale kites and playing with whale toys, and wishing Pheena the best birthday and bon voyage possible. We had national coverage, including *National Geographic.*

We won a lot of converts that day, and I'm sure that Pheena is continuing to win hearts all over America. Besides all that, nobody got squished.

BERKELEY AND THE BARD

Berkeley, California, is known for a number of things, but its Shakespeare Festival was not one of them until recently. Seven years ago, a small group of actors began performing Shakespeare in the city's John Hinkel park, a lovely outdoor amphitheater in the Berkeley Hills. Devotees of the Bard come to the park, picnic basket and bottle of wine in hand (and a thermos of coffee to fend off the foggy evening chill), and settle onto the theater's terraces to watch Shakespeare's magic come to life.

The performances are wonderful. Critics and Shakespearean scholars had discovered the small festival, and lots of good things were written about it in learned journals. Unfortunately, most people read the *Daily News,* not the *Shakespeare Quarterly,* and the small company was struggling to make ends meet. A full house was a rarity. Let's set the stage for handling BSF's PR. The following will probably be helpful to any small arts organizations. It can be applied, in one way or another, to dance, music, or any other performing art.

The Actors: Literally, actors. Plus a good Board of Directors and dedicated volunteers.

The Goal: To make the public aware of the Festival, and to fill the house.

The Method:

One of the first problems we had to face was ill will from the neighbors and a cool reception at City Hall. Because the theater is out-of-doors in a residential area, the neighbors had some legitimate complaints about noise and parking. We also had some minor problems with both city and county government, which in the past had boiled over into the local newspapers, making matters even worse.

In each case, a committee was delegated to sit down and work things out, rather than to confront. A couple of neighborhood residents were added to the Board of Directors. By the time the season started, noise and traffic were well under control, being handled by Festival volunteers, and the City fathers and mothers were pleased as punch that we were in the park.

However, another problem was lurking in the wings. California's Proposition 13 had cut the funding out from under everything, including the arts. The corporations were tightening their belts as well. And, the lion's share of donations were going to already-established theater groups, which left us out in the cold. The group had credentials from the critics, but not from the general public.

As a result, the publicity campaign became even more important. For the Festival to survive, it would have to make it big at the box office. And there was very little money for advertising. We also needed to establish the Festival's credibility with the general public once and for all, to ensure future funding.

Our game plan was ambitious, and included scraping, scrounging, begging, borrowing, and relying on the good graces of a great many people. We would run billboards, radio *and* television PSAs, schedule heavily on talk shows, obtain moderate news coverage, and go for major coverage in the Sunday entertainment pages. Of course, the usual calendar announcements would have to go out, press lists be specially prepared, and myriad other minor details attended to.

The time schedule called for early prepublicity to help boost subscription sales. We didn't do too well in this area for a number of reasons: among them, a shortage of black and white photos appropriate for releases, and a general lack of interest on the part of talk show hosts to schedule a March interview for something that was happening in July. Finally, because of the extensive nature of the actual PR campaign and the limited time and funds available to accomplish it, we simply didn't have time to stage the types of news events that would normally bring the press out.

We also didn't have time to cry over spilt milk, and continued working on the materials that we expected to make us famous. The idea was to create an image of the Festival, to have something identifiable in all of our printed materials that would jog people's memory whenever they saw it. We found a terrific photo of one of our actors playing Oberon in the previous season's performance of "A Midsummer Night's Dream." He was a stern and compelling Oberon, and that face staring down from a billboard was going to get attention. We had negotiated free billboard space with Foster & Kleiser, and they were gracious enough to add the services of a very capable graphic artist as well. That left us with printing and labor costs. Fortunately, Foster & Kleiser employees became enamoured of the Festival, and we traded tickets for labor costs. We got a great deal on printing from a local printer.

We had chosen our locations carefully—two billboards in San Francisco: one in the theater districts and one in the financial district, and the others on main thoroughfares in Berkeley, Oakland, and Marin County.

The talk shows began about six weeks before the Festival opened. Four weeks before, the TV and radio PSAs began running, and continued to run for the duration of the Festival, along with the talk shows. Our print ads, featuring the same Oberon as our billboard, began running. And the week before the Festival opened, we got the cover of the Sunday magazine.

By opening night, subscriptions were double what they had been the previous year, and after the first rave reviews on "The Merry Wives of Windsor" appeared, we sold out every single performance of all three productions.

We wiped out a deficit from the previous year, and ended up with a little money ahead for the next season. We initially kept a record of where people had heard about the Festival, but it soon became more cumbersome than helpful. Basically, every person asked had seen the billboard, heard a PSA or talk show, or whatever. The publicity had done just what we wanted. It had created an overall image for people to identify and it had reinforced itself.

Prospective patrons of the arts, of course, should not cease their activities because the Berkeley Shakespeare Festival did well at the box office and didn't have to spend much to do it. First of all, we did have some funding. Secondly, we had one of the best and most professional volunteer staffs I have ever seen, which is highly unusual. We were able to accomplish a lot because we had a lot of professional talent at our fingertips that an arts organization would normally pay through the nose for. To wit: publicity services were volunteered, as were those of a professional graphic artist, a professional journalist, a CPA to do our books, an attorney specializing in the arts, a professional designer and architect, a professional camera crew who filmed the PSA for TV on their own time and at their own expense, and the space and services provided by Foster and Kleiser. In addition, we obtained a number of other services at minimal cost.

This is highly unusual, and not many other organizations have this kind of talent in its volunteer ranks. So don't put the checkbook away. All facets of the performing arts community need all of the help they can get.

Talk show possibilities were great. Our directors and actors and actresses were all extremely cooperative with the PR campaign, and willingly appeared on both television and radio, (more professionals) as did the festival's draumaturge and the president of our Board of Directors. Subject matter ranged from what kind of a gourmet picnic one could take to the philosophical implications of "King Lear" for today's world, to why in the world a black actor would get into Shakespeare. We scheduled approximately 30 talk shows or TV appearances within a six-week period, and the subject was never the same.

A friend had been working with a group of electronic media types producing PSAs for TV that actually got a lot of air time. They agreed to produce our entire spot.

We also did well with print media. We had a wonderful secret weapon in the person of our president of the Board, who just happens to be a professor of journalism, who just happens to have trained about half the editors and reporters in the Bay Area. All I needed for print coverage was to turn him loose on his former students.

Also, the Festival's General Manager made a wise decision by agreeing to concentrate PR efforts on the plays. The Festival has a number of other programs besides the plays, that also need PR attention. Rather than do a so-so job on everything, we did a bang-up job on what was most important at the time.

As a result of a good PR campaign and a lot of hard work by a lot of people, the Bard is alive and well in Berkeley!

NURSING HOMES—AN AMERICAN TRAGEDY.

If "King Lear" was the great tragedy of Shakespearean England, nursing homes are most assuredly the great tragedy of modern America.

I first became aware of the problem while working with California Citizen Action Group (CalCag, now United Neighbors in Action), an organization concerned with consumer issues. We had received several anonymous phone calls regarding the fact that patients in certain nursing homes were being mistreated to the point of dying from negligence.

Finally, a couple of people came forward to meet with us. One man's wife had been in a nursing home for two years. Whenever he complained about the treatment she was receiving, he would find new bruises on his spouse at the next visit. He, like many other families with loved ones in these home, had learned to keep his mouth shut. But it had proven too much. He had managed to slip in a camera, and the pictures he brought out were unbelievable. He had also kept an accurate, day-by-day journal, which proved helpful in the long run.

We had just touched the tip of the iceberg on what was to be one of the most difficult projects I've ever worked on, both emotionally and publicity-wise. In the end, I dropped out because I felt that my emotions had gotten in the way of good judgment. It is difficult to watch people who are helpless be mistreated.

Publicity would have been no problem if CalCag had a membership of hardhearted sensationalists. We could have released photos that would have turned the stomach of the public, and created such a sense of outrage that the nursing homes would have been razed with their managerial staff in them. Thus would have done little to solve the problem overall, and would have created a number of hardships for patients then in the homes and their families.

Our basic publicity problem was that nobody was willing to step forward and speak publicly. Families had already experienced the pain of having their verbal complaints result in physical retaliation against the patient. Those who came to us made it clear that their names could not be used. The nurse's aides who supported the families' claims were in danger of losing their jobs, so their identities had to be protected as well. We basically found ourselves in a situation where we had two possible alternatives: first, to create press possibilities, and second, to pounce on every opportunity that we could to gain coverage without endangering patients.

There were additional problems. The state agencies in charge of regulating the homes were more than recalcitrant. They were almost unwilling to listen to complaints from any quarter. More than once we were told that "You can't really pay any attention to the mutterings of old people—they are usually senile." The credibility of our sources was constantly questioned.

We decided that we would have to create a basis to go public. In order to do this, several CalCag members, including yours truly, became visiting angels from God. We set ourselves up as a religious group who wanted to visit the patients. We returned from our first visit with emotions ranging from depression to a barely restrained desire to commit premeditated murder. You expect such conditions in a prison or a refugee camp, not in what is supposedly a medical facilities for the elderly.

After a calming down period of several days, we put our information together, selected our speakers, and began hitting the talk show circuit. The results were overwhelming. We began receiving calls from families who had come close to the limits of human endurance over the treatment that a relative was receiving at the hands these homes. We received calls from concerned citizens who wanted to get involved. And, in a way what was most important, the authorities finally realized that they had better start paying attention to the situation.

We approached the State Department of Health, and armed with grievances, which by now were well documented, we asked for surprise inspections of two of the worst offenders, and asked that members of our organization be allowed to go along. Several mornings later we got a call to meet the health inspectors at one of the homes.

In the past, the homes had often received word ahead of time that the inspectors were coming, and had cleaned up their act. This time, there was no such warning, and approximately 83 citations were issued against the home, including two class A infractions, which meant that bodily harm or death had resulted from negligence on the part of the hospital.

We called a press conference for the following morning—no time to send announcements. I simply sat down at the telephone and began calling assignment editors. Every major media outlet, including the wires, covered the conference. Public outrage began to assert itself. Elected officials began receiving phone calls from irate constituents, and the CalCag office was flooded with calls, some offering help and services, others further documenting abuses. More surprise inspections were held and more citations were issued to other nursing homes.

This type of issue is usually ongoing, and the nursing home issue is no exception. CalCag has now become United Neighbors in Action, and deals exclusively with the plight of the elderly in nursing homes. Even so, the problem still exists, and long-term solutions don't seem to be forthcoming.

The nursing home industry has clout. Some key government officials were removed from their posts because they had pushed too hard for reform. However, the public is now aware of the problem, and as more people become involved, we come closer to a solution.

Meanwhile, patient treatment has probably improved somewhat. It should also be noted that we found nursing homes affiliated with churches—especially Catholic and Jewish—to be excellent for the most part. We can only hope that the public will continue to fight what may well be one of the most abusive industries in America. We hope that the skills presented in this book can help other communities deal with similar problems.

A SINGLE-ISSUE CONSTITUENCY PRESS KIT: THE BERKELEY SHAKESPEARE FESTIVAL.

Press Release
History of the Festival (Background)
Season's Offerings (Basically, a fact sheet)
Black and white photo, backed.

At each opening night performance, the press kit was updated. The release covered the play in question and a new photo of the current production was included. A biography on the director replaced the season's offerings (no longer necessary). The background sheet was left in.

FOR IMMEDIATE
RELEASE   CONTACT: Judy Kimsey
                                 Michael Hardesty

SHAKESPEARE IN THE PARK—THE BARD IS ALIVE AND WELL IN BERKELEY.

Shakespeare is alive and thriving in Berkeley's John Hinkel Park, where the faithful gather every summer—picnic baskets and wine in hand—for what is rapidly becoming one of the top Shakespearean festivals in the country.

The ritual begins an hour or so before the performance. The revellers arrive with the first wisps of summer fog, spreading blankets on the outdoor amphitheater's terraces, and enjoying leisurely dinners and conversation with friends. As the dusk finally settles onto the hills, and the audience settles in with a glass of good wine, the stage becomes peopled with characters from Shakespeare's teeming world—and the play begins.

This season opens with *The Merry Wives of Windsor,* a rollicking comedy originally commissioned by Queen Elizabeth I. The Berkeley festival's offering will feature original Elizabethan music, and will be directed by Richard White, award-winning director from Eureka Theater.

The second play is *The Tempest,* Shakespeare's last play and one of his most magical and poetic achievements. The wooded amphitheatre provides a superb setting for this production, which will be directed by Audrey Stanley, who has also directed at the Ashland Festival.

The season closes with *King Lear,* a tragedy which, more than any other, probes into the very essence of the human condition. Julian Lopez-Morillas, whose direction of *Pericles* took the Bay Area Critics Circle award for Outstanding Direction, will direct *Lear.*

The Berkeley Shakespeare Festival stresses a swift, direct and eloquent style in both production and performance, with emphasis on a strong and lucid interpretive line of movement throughout the text.

The Festival runs from July 9 through September 28, Subscriptions are recommended because of the amphitheatre's small seating capacity. For more information, or to subscribe, call 845-0303.

-30-

FEATURE EDITORS AND TALK SHOW HOSTS: Our actors, directors, and dramaturg are all available for interviews, as are several of the neighborhood children who are learning Shakespeare by attending the park rehersals. For more information, or to set up an interview, please contact Judy Kimsey, 398-6363.

Background Information, The Berkeley Shakespeare Festival.

Founded in 1974, the Berkeley Shakespeare Festival is the only professional Shakespeare company in Northern California. Our productions are designed to enchant the uninitiated, as well as to meet the criteria of the most demanding critics and scholars. We have succeeded. Not only do our productions draw praise from critics throughout the country, they also attract and are understood by children. Many youngsters in the vicinity of the Park have been drawn into Shakespeare's world, and now recite entire passages by heart.

Performances take place throughout the summer, in John Hinkel Park's outdoor amphitheater. The actors use a simple platform stage with an adjustable second level. The audience, seated on a steep, terraced hillside, maintains a direct and intimate relationship with the players. The atmosphere is informal, and the audience is diverse, including scholars, families, and those seeing their first Shakespearean production.

The style of production and performance emphasizes the clarity of the spoken word, and a strong, lucid, interpretive line of movement throughout the text. It is style that is swift, direct, and eloquent. While we do not do Shakespeare solemnly, neither do we go to the all-too-fashionable extreme of forcing a modern angle.

Last year, more than 15,000 people attended performances in John Hinkel Park, and many more saw the company on tour at Davis, Santa Cruz, the Mondavi Winery in Napa, and at San Francisco's Golden Gate Park.

The 1980 Season: Berkeley Shakespeare Festival

The Merry Wives Of Windsor, July 9 through August 3.

This is a farce that was apocryphally commissioned by Queen Elizabeth I, so that she could see Falstaff in love. It has good parts for women, which is one reason the Festival has chosen to present it. *Merry Wives* is hilarious when done properly— that is, when the comedy is kept fresh, the tone light, and the plot clear—which is how we intend to do it.

Richard White, award-winning director from Eureka Theater will direct *Merry Wives,* and Eliza Chugg will create the costumes. Original Elizabethan music will be used in the production.

The Tempest, August 6 through August 31.

The Festival has a special affinity for Shakespeare's late romances—those delicate plays of reconciliation and redemption —such as *The Tempest.* Audrey Stanley, a member of the Theater Arts Department at U.C. Berkeley, and a past director at the Ashland Festival, will direct. Her conception is to bring out the deep humanity, as well as the magic, of the work.

The Tempest also lends itself superbly to our park setting. Costume designer is Douglas Russell, and Stephen Thewlis will create an original score for the production.

King Lear, September 3 through September 28.

This tragedy, more than any other, probes into the very essence of the human condition, commemorating (in the words of Alfred Harbage), "humanity's long, agonized and continuing struggle to be human."

The Festival has waited for six years to do *Lear,* steadily developing the depth in the acting company that is required to present a play demanding perhaps the greatest constellation of characters in Elizabethan drama.

Julian Lopez-Morillas, whose direction of last year's *Pericles* received awards and commendations from many critics, will direct *Lear,* and Stephen Thewlis will create the original score to be used in the play.

Stage settings for all three productions will be created by Ron Pratt and Gene Angell, who have won numerous awards for their spectacular settings.

Au Revoir From the Authors

When we began writing this book, we had little idea that it would be so timely. We are living in an era of budget cuts and general "unfunding" of the arts and the nonprofit sectors. Unfortunately, things are likely to get worse before they get better.

Now, more than ever, the talents of a publicist are required to keep the cause—whatever it may be—in the public eye. The fact that government sees fit to ignore various problems doesn't mean that they will go away. Old people are still freezing to death or starving to death because they are neglected; children are still being abused; our natural resources are still diminishing; small businesses continue to suffer at the expense of larger businesses; and the arts still receive less government funding in this, the richest country in the world, than in almost any other country.

We hope that the tools we have given you will serve as a basis for creating new techniques in publicity, as well as for providing a framework for current projects.

Finally, we hope that we have saved harried reporters and editors a small headache by eliminating the ten-page, single-spaced press release.

Do-gooders of the world, unite—and good luck!